Doggin' Northwest Florida

The 50 Best Places To Hike With Your Dog In The Panhandle

DOUG GELBERT

illustrations by

ANDREW CHESWORTH

Cruden Bay Books

There is always a new trail to look forward to...

DOGGIN' NORTHWEST FLORIDA: THE 50 BEST PLACES
TO HIKE WITH YOUR DOG IN THE PANHANDLE

Copyright 2008 by Cruden Bay Books

Cruden Bay Books
PO Box 467
Montchanin, DE 19710
www.hikewithyourdog.com

International Standard Book Number 978-0-9815346-1-9

*"Dogs are our link to paradise...to sit with a dog on a hillside
on a glorious afternoon is to be back in Eden,
where doing nothing was not boring - it was peace."*
- Milan Kundera

Ahead On The Trail

No Dogs!   14

The 50 Best Places To Hike With Your Dog   15

Camping With Your Dog   104

Your Dog At The Beach   115

Index To Parks, Trails And Open Space   116

Also...

Hiking With Your Dog   5

Outfitting Your Dog For A Hike   9

Low Impact Hiking With Your Dog   12

Introduction

Northwest Florida can be a great place to hike with your dog. Within a short drive your canine adventurer can be climbing seaside dunes that leave him panting, trotting in rolling pinelands, exploring the estates of America's wealthiest families or circling lakes for miles and never lose sight of the water.

I have selected what I consider to be the 50 best places to take your dog for an outing in Northwest Florida and ranked them according to subjective criteria including the variety of hikes available, opportunities for canine swimming and pleasure of the walks. The rankings include a mix of parks that feature long walks and parks that contain short walks. Did I miss your favorite? Let us know at ***www.hikewithyourdog. com.***

For dog owners it is important to realize that not all parks are open to our best trail companions (see page 14 for a list of parks that do not allow dogs). It is sometimes hard to believe but not everyone loves dogs. We are, in fact, in the minority when compared with our non-dog owning neighbors.

So when visiting a park always keep your dog under control and clean up any messes and we can all expect our great parks to remain open to our dogs. And maybe some others will see the light as well. *Remember, every time you go out with your dog you are an ambassador for all dog owners.*

Grab that leash and hit the trail!
DBG

Hiking With Your Dog

So you want to start hiking with your dog. Hiking with your dog can be a fascinating way to explore the Florida Panhandle from a canine perspective. Some things to consider:

🐾 Dog's Health

Hiking can be a wonderful preventative for any number of physical and behavioral disorders. One in every three dogs is overweight and running up trails and leaping through streams is great exercise to help keep pounds off. Hiking can also relieve boredom in a dog's routine and calm dogs prone to destructive habits. And hiking with your dog strengthens the overall owner/dog bond.

🐾 Breed of Dog

All dogs enjoy the new scents and sights of a trail. But some dogs are better suited to hiking than others. If you don't as yet have a hiking companion, select a breed that matches your interests. Do you look forward to an entire afternoon's hiking? You'll need a dog bred to keep up with such a pace, such as a retriever or a spaniel. Is a half-hour enough walking for you? It may not be for an energetic dog like a border collie. If you already have a hiking friend, tailor your plans to his abilities.

🐾 Conditioning

Just like humans, dogs need to be acclimated to the task at hand. An inactive dog cannot be expected to bounce from the easy chair in the den to complete a 3-hour hike. You must also be physically able to restrain your dog if confronted with distractions on the trail (like a scampering squirrel or a pack of joggers). Have your dog checked by a veterinarian before significantly increasing his activity level.

🐾 Weather

Hot humid Florida summers do not do dogs any favors. With no sweat glands and only panting available to disperse body heat, dogs are much more susceptible to heat stroke than we are. Unusually rapid panting and/or a bright red tongue are signs of heat exhaustion in your pet.

Always carry enough water for your hike. Even the prime hiking days of late fall through early spring that don't seem too warm can cause discomfort in dark-coated dogs if the sun is shining brightly. During cold snaps, short-coated breeds may require additional attention.

🐾 Trail Hazards

Dogs won't get poison ivy but they can transfer it to you. Some trails are littered with small pieces of broken glass that can slice a dog's paws. Nasty thorns can also blanket trails that we in shoes may never notice. At the beach beware of sand spurs that can often be present in scrubby, sandy areas.

🐾 Ticks

You won't be able to spend much time in Florida woods without encountering ticks. All are nasty but the deer tick - no bigger than a pin head - carries with it the spectre of Lyme disease. Lyme disease attacks a dog's joints and makes walking painful. The tick needs to be embedded in the skin to transmit Lyme disease. It takes 4-6 hours for a tick to become embedded and another 24-48 hours to transmit Lyme disease bacteria.

When hiking, walk in the middle of trails away from tall grass and bushes. And when the summer sun fades away don't stop thinking about ticks - they remain active any time the temperature is above 30 degrees. By checking your dog - and yourself - thoroughly after each walk you can help avoid Lyme disease. Ticks tend to congregate on your dog's ears, between the toes and around the neck and head.

🐾 Water

Surface water, including fast-flowing streams, is likely to be infested with a microscopic protozoa called *Giardia*, waiting to wreak havoc on a dog's intestinal system. The most common symptom is crippling diarrhea. Algae, pollutants and contaminants can all be in streams, ponds and puddles. If possible, carry fresh water for your dog on the trail - your dog can even learn to drink happily from a squirt bottle.

At the beach, cool sea water will be tempting for your dog but try to limit any drinking as much as possible. Again, have plenty of fresh water available for your dog to drink instead.

🐾 Rattlesnakes and Copperheads, etc.

Rattlesnakes and their close cousins, copperheads, are not particularly aggressive animals but you should treat any venomous snake with respect and keep your distance. A rattler's colors may vary but they are recognized by the namesake rattle on the tail and a diamond-shaped head. Unless cornered or teased by humans or dogs, a rattlesnake will crawl away and avoid striking. Avoid placing your hand in unexamined rocky areas and crevasses and try and keep your dog from doing so as well. Stick to the trail and out of high grass where you can't see well. If you hear a nearby rattle, stop immediately and hold your dog back. Identify where the snake is and slowly back away.

If you or your dog is bitten, do not panic but get to a hospital or veterinarian with as little physical movement as possible. Wrap between the bite and the heart. Rattlesnakes might give "dry bites" where no poison is injected, but you should always check with a doctor after a bite even if you feel fine.

🐾 Black Bears

Are you likely to see a bear while out hiking with your dog? No, it's not likely. It is, however, quite a thrill if you are fortunate enough to spot a black bear on the trail - from a distance.

Black bear attacks are incredibly rare. In the year 2000 a hiker was killed by a black bear in Great Smoky National Park and it was the first deadly bear attack in the 66-year history of America's most popular national park. It was the first EVER in the southeastern United States. In all of North America only 43 black bear mauling deaths have ever been recorded (through 1999).

Most problems with black bears occur near a campground (like the above incident) where bears have learned to forage for unprotected food. On the trail bears will typically see you and leave the area. What should you do if you encounter a black bear? Experts agree on three important things:

1) Never run. A bear will outrun you, outclimb you, outswim you. Don't look like prey.
2) Never get between a female bear and a cub who may be nearby feeding.
3) Leave a bear an escape route.

If the bear is at least 15 feet away and notices you make sure you keep your dog close and calm. If a bear stands on its hind legs or comes closer it may just be trying to get a better view or smell to evaluate the situation. Wave your arms and make noise to scare the bear away. Most bears will quickly leave the area.

If you encounter a black bear at close range, stand upright and make yourself appear as large a foe as possible. Avoid direct eye contact and speak in a calm, assertive and assuring voice as you back up slowly and out of danger.

Alligators

Alligators are found in marshes, swamps, rivers and lakes as well as neighborhood drainage ditches and canals - anywhere you see water is potential gator habitat. Use common sense and do not not allow your dog in waters where alligators may be lurking. Don't walk your dog close to water if you can avoid it.

If you see an alligator on land, just walk your dog away from the area - although they can scurry 30 miles per hour for short distances, alligators do not run down prey on land. They may run on land to escape danger or protect a nest but will not come after you if there is an escape route to the water. Make sure you give him one.

Outfitting Your Dog For A Hike

These are the basics for taking your dog on a hike:

▸ **Collar.**
A properly fitting collar should not be so loose as to come off but you should be able to slide your flat hand under the collar.

▸ **Identification Tags.**
Get one with your veterinarian's phone number as well.

▸ **Bandanna.**
Can help distinguish him from game in hunting season.

▸ **Leash.**
Leather lasts forever but if there's water in your dog's future, consider quick-drying nylon.

▸ **Water.**
Carry 8 ounces for every hour of hiking.

🐾 *I want my dog to help carry water, snacks and other supplies on the trail. Where do I start?*
To select an appropriate dog pack measure your dog's girth around the rib cage. A dog pack should fit securely without hindering the dog's ability to walk normally.

🐾 *Will my dog wear a pack?*
Wearing a dog pack is no more obtrusive than wearing a collar, although some dogs will take to a pack easier than others. Introduce the pack by draping a towel over your dog's back in the house and then having your dog wear an empty pack on short walks. Progressively add some crumpled newspaper and then bits of clothing. Fill the pack with treats and reward your dog from the stash. Soon your dog will associate the dog pack with an outdoor adventure and will eagerly look forward to wearing it.

How much weight can I put into a dog pack?

Many dog packs are sold by weight recommendations. A healthy, well-conditioned dog can comfortably carry 25% to 33% of its body weight. Breeds prone to back problems or hip dysplasia should not wear dog packs. Consult your veterinarian before stuffing the pouches with gear.

How does a dog wear a pack?

The pack, typically with cargo pouches on either side, should ride as close to the shoulders as possible without limiting movement. The straps that hold the dog pack in place should be situated where they will not cause chafing.

What are good things to put in a dog pack?

Low density items such as food and poop bags are good choices. Ice cold bottles of water can cool your dog down on hot days. Don't put anything in a dog pack that can break. Dogs will bang the pack on rocks and trees as they wiggle through tight spots in the trail. Dogs also like to lie down in creeks and other wet spots so seal items in plastic bags. A good use for dog packs when on day hikes around Northwest Florida is trail maintenance - your dog can pack out trash left by inconsiderate visitors before you.

🐾 *Are dog booties a good idea?*

Although not typically necessary, dog booties can be an asset, especially for the occasional canine hiker whose paw pads have not become toughened. Most Florida trails are soft under paw but in some places there may be broken glass or roots. Hiking boots for dogs are designed to prevent pads from cracking while trotting across rough surfaces.

🐾 *What should a doggie first aid kit include?*

Even when taking short hikes it is a good idea to have some basics available for emergencies:

- ▶ 4" square gauze pads
- ▶ cling type bandaging tapes
- ▶ topical wound disinfectant cream
- ▶ tweezers
- ▶ insect repellent - no reason to leave your dog unprotected against mosquitoes and biting flies
- ▶ veterinarian's phone number

"I can't think of anything that brings me closer to tears than
when my old dog - completely exhausted after a hard day
in the field - limps away from her nice spot in front of the fire
and comes over to where I'm sitting and puts her head in my lap,
a paw over my knee, and closes her eyes, and goes back to sleep.
I don't know what I've done to deserve that kind of friend."
-Gene Hill

Low Impact Hiking
With Your Dog

Every time you hike with your dog on the trail you are an ambassador for all dog owners. Some people you meet won't believe in your right to take a dog on the trail. Be friendly to all and make the best impression you can by practicing low impact hiking with your dog:

- Pack out everything you pack in.

- Do not leave dog scat on the trail; if you haven't brought plastic bags for poop removal bury it away from the trail and topical water sources.

- Hike only where dogs are allowed.

- Stay on the trail.

- Do not allow your dog to chase wildlife.

- Step off the trail and wait with your dog while horses and other hikers pass.

- Do not allow your dog to bark - people are enjoying the trail for serenity.

- *Have as much fun on your hike as your dog does.*

The Other End Of The Leash

Leash laws are like speed limits - everyone seems to have a private interpretation of their validity. Some dog owners never go outside with an unleashed dog; others treat the laws as suggestions or disregard them completely. It is not the purpose of this book to tell dog owners where to go to evade the leash laws or reveal the parks where rangers will look the other way at an unleashed dog. Nor is it the business of this book to preach vigilant adherence to the leash laws. Nothing written in a book is going to change people's behavior with regard to leash laws. So this will be the last time leash laws are mentioned, save occasionally when we point out the parks where dogs are welcomed off leash.

Visiting Florida State Parks

State park pet rules: "Pets are permitted in designated day-use areas at ALL Florida State Parks. They must be kept on a hand-held leash that is six-feet or shorter and be well-behaved at all times. Pet owners are required to pick up after their pets and properly dispose of their droppings. Pets are not permitted on beaches or playgrounds, or in bathing areas, cabins, park buildings, or concession facilities."

State forests and wildlife management areas in Florida allow hunting. If you can only hike with your dog in such places during hunting season, outfit yourself and your dog in blaze orange and stick to the trails. Hunting season coincides with prime hiking season after September but often is restricted to specific days of the week so plan your dog's outings accordingly.

No Dogs

Before we get started on the best places to take your dog, let's get out of the way some of the parks that do not allow dogs at all:

Apalachicola Bluffs and Ravines Preserve

Eglin Air Force Base

Perdido Key State Park

St. Vincent National Wildlife Refuge

O.K. that wasn't too bad. Let's forget about these and move on to some of the great places where we CAN take our dogs on Northwest Florida trails...

The 50 Best Places
To Hike With Your Dog
In Northwest Florida...

1
Torreya
State Park

The Park

Hardy Bryan Croom, a planter and naturalist of some renown, began amassing land in northern Florida in the 1820s and in 1833 purchased 640 acres of the Lafayette Land Grant for what would become Goodwood Plantation. While exploring from his cotton plantation, Croom discovered one of the rarest conifers in the world along the banks of the Apalachicola River. He named the small evergreen "torreya" after the botanist Dr. John Torrey.

It would turn out the torreya was native to only five other spots in the world - one in California, four in Japan and China, and on the bluffs of the Apalachicola. Croom's own botanical career would be cut short in 1837 when he perished with 89 others aboard the *S.S. Home* off the coast of Cape Hatteras in the Racer's Storm, one of the most destructive hurricanes of the 19th century.

During the Great Depression, workers in President Franklin Roosevelt's "Tree Army," the Civilian Conservation Corps, developed the park.

Liberty

Phone Number
- (850) 643-2674

Website
- floridastateparks.org/torreya

Admission Fee
- Vehicle parking fee

Park Hours
- 8:00 a.m. to sunset

Directions
- *Rock Bluff*; from Exit 174 off I-10, head south on SR 12. Turn right on CR 1641 and continue to the park entrance at the end.

The Walks

On the way to nowhere, your dog will thank you for making the special trip to Torreya State Park. This is the best one-hour workout your dog can get in Northwest Florida, hiking across terrain more familiar in Appalachian foothills. Indeed, the mix of hardwoods thriving at the various elevations in the park conspire to whip up Florida's best display of autumn colors.

There are two hiking loops at Torreya, each about seven miles around. Along the Apalachicola River the *Rock Bluff Trail* dips and rolls through ravines with some climbs that may set your dog to panting. Several park roads and connecting trails can be used to dissect this loop into manageable chunks.

That is not the case with the *Torreya Challenge* in the eastern section of the park. Once you cross the stone bridge with your dog you won't see the trailhead again for several hours. Your dog will think she has left Florida on this scenic ramble.

This is the only place your dog will see the rare torreya tree. Mature trees can still be seen in the park, especially in ravines. These saplings are being raised in captivity.

Trail Sense: There are mapboards at the parking lot and the trails are reliably blazed.

Dog Friendliness
Dogs are permitted on the trails and allowed in the campground where poop bags are provided, but can not go in the Yurt area.
Traffic
Don't expect much of it - serious trail users only need apply.
Canine Swimming
Streams you encounter are best suited for splashing.
Trail Time
Several hours.

2
Topsail Hill Preserve State Park

The Park

Topsail Hill is the most intact coastal ecosystem in all of Florida. The state moved to protect this unique natural area by purchasing 1,637 acres here in 1992. There are 14 identifiable ecosystems, including freshwater coastal dune lakes, wet prairies, scrub, pine flatwoods, marshes, cypress domes, seepage slopes and 3.2 miles white sand beaches - the remnants of quartz washed down from the Appalachian Mountains.

Topsail Hill gets its name from the landmark 25-foot high dune that resembles a ship's topsail.

The Walks

Topsail Hill is the best place that you can take your dog for an extended hike along the Gulf of Mexico. The

Walton

Phone Number
- (850) 267-0299

Website
- www.floridastateparks.org/topsailhill/default.cfm

Admission Fee
- Vehicle entrance fee

Park Hours
- 8:00 a.m. to sunset

Directions
- *Santa Rosa Beach*; the main entrance is on CR 30A, one mile east of US 98, but the entrance of choice for most dog owners will be via Topsail Road from US 98, west of the junction with CR 30A.

trail of choice is the *Morris Lake Nature Trail*, a 2.5-mile balloon route laid out through ancient coastal dunes. The dunes trail is wide open and exposed to the elements so bring plenty of water for your dog on a hot day and since every step of the way is across glistening white soft sugar sand, your dog will get a workout any time of the year. In fact, look for iron tracks laid down during World War II that allowed heavy trucks to travel across the thick sand when these dunes were used as a bombing range.

Morris Lake is one of three freshwater coastal dune lakes on the property. These rare oases are found only along the Gulf Coast in America and while tempting to visit for your dog, are inhabited by alligators. The trail climbs briefly into a Florida shrub community where your dog can find some shade among the sand pines and shrubby oaks before finishing along the Gulf of Mexico beach.

If your dog isn't spent from an hour on the Morris Lake dunes there is more hiking available in the other direction to Campbell Lake. This trail can also be accessed from the main entrance and campground and your dog won't be allowed to finish the entire 5.2-mile loop (it tracks along the beach) but she can reach the broad, flat lakeside.

Trail Sense: A trailmap and interpretive brochure can be found at the trailhead and directional signs decipher the faceless dunes.

Dog Friendliness
Dogs are allowed on the trails and in the campground but not on the beach

Traffic
Foot traffic only and you won't encounter many casual strollers deep into the dune system.

Canine Swimming
Alligators live in the lake but your dog can step in to cool off.

Trail Time
Several hours.

Your dog will find the best dunesland hiking on the Gulf Coast at Topsail Hill Preserve.

3
Leon Sinks
Geological Area

The Park

Leon Sinks is in the heart of the Woodville Karst Plain, a vast area of porous limestone bedrock that stetches for 450 square miles from Tallahassee south to the Gulf of Mexico. The terrain is shaped by rain and groundwater that dissolve the limestone to form sinkholes, swales and underground caverns. The limestone was formed millions of years ago from ancient coral reefs and shell deposits.

Above ground Leon Sinks is administered by the Apalachicola National Forest. The karst plain is still evolving; acidic water continues to dissolve underlying limestone and when cavities become large enough, the surface layer collapses and new sinkholes can form at any time.

Leon
Phone Number - (850) 926-3561
Website - www.fs.fed.us/r8/florida/ recreation/index_apa.shtml
Admission Fee - Parking fee required
Park Hours - 8:00 a.m. to 8:00 p.m.
Directions - *Tallahassee*; seven miles south of the city on the west side of US 319.

The Walks

The trail system at Leon Sinks is a four-mile loop that links the *Sinkhole Trail* and the *Gunswamp Trail* (sinkholes are formed by the underwater aquifer, swamps are created by surface water). A *Crossover Trail* separates the two into a stacked-loop for canine hikers who don't want to experience the entirety of this vibrant community.

The *Sinkhole Trail* connects more than a dozen sinkholes, some dry and some filled with water. Boardwalk observation decks provide close-up views. The deepest is the Big Dismal Sink at 130 feet. Keep a close hold on your dog around these sinks - they have steep walls and dogs - and people - have drowned at Leon Sinks.

Except for traffic noise you can't ever quite shake, this is one of the best hikes you can take with your dog in Northwest Florida. From the tupelo gum swamps to the sandy ridges you cannot find a more diverse plant world along the trail. At Big Dismal Sink alone more than 75 different plants cascade down the sink's conical walls.

Your dog will savor the airy wiregrass community on the sandy ridges at Leon Sinks Geological Area.

None of the underground limestone penetrates the ground so the trails are paw-friendly sand and a joy for your dog.

Trail Sense: Maps are available and the trail is marked and signed at junctions.

Dog Friendliness

Dogs are welcome to hike at Leon Sinks and they keep a plastic water bowl at the trailhead water fountain for a hot, thirsty trail dog.

Traffic

Foot traffic only and light visitation.

Canine Swimming

No.

Trail Time

More than one hour.

4
St. Marks
National Wildlife Refuge

The Park

St. Marks NWR was established in 1931 for wintering migratory birds, and over 300 species of birds have been recorded on the refuge, with 98 species nesting on-site. There are 14 active bald eagle nests spread across the park's 68,000 acres. St. Marks includes coastal marshes, islands, tidal creeks and the estuaries of seven Florida rivers.

The Walks

Dogs are not allowed on most national park trails and one of the reasons given is that they might harass wildlife. Yet dog are often permitted on the trails in national wildlife refuges - and that is the happy case at St. Marks.

Wakulla/Jefferson

Phone Number
- (850) 925-6121

Website
- www.fws.gov/saintmarks

Admission Fee
- Vehicle parking fee

Park Hours
- 8:00 a.m. to sunset

Directions
- *St. Marks*; at the end of SR 59, three miles south of US 98, east of Newport.

The star walk for canine day hikers is the *Mounds Pool Interpretive Trail* that dips in and out of woods around freshwater and salt marshes. Highlights include close-up looks at Cabbage Palms, the Florida state tree. At the lighthouse the *Levee Trail* and *Cedar Point Trail* introduce more hardy plants adapting to the whipping winds and salt spray. Your dog will only have to deal with the potentially harsh conditions for about one mile.

There are several other short trails to sample on the St. Marks Unit or you can pull the car off to side and create your own routes on the open levees and old logging roads. You can wander for hours on these primitive walking trails and not see another trail user.

Nearly 50 miles of the *Florida National Scenic Trail* snakes through the wildlife refuge, traversing a greater variety of forest types and wildlife communities than any other North Florida stretch of the cross-state trail. In addition to several miles in the St. Marks Unit, you can travel west on US 98 to the

Wakulla Unit and the Panacea Unit, each of which also have several miles of the *Florida Trail*.

Trail Sense: There are maps, signs, brochures and trail markings to help you navigate the 75 miles of trail here.

Dog Friendliness
Dogs are allowed to use the refuge trails.

Traffic
Foot traffic only on the *Florida Trail* sections; horses and bikes are permitted on the primitive road/trails.

Canine Swimming
Alligators thrive in the ponds and pools around the refuge levees; the area is marshy but there is access to the Gulf of Mexico near the lighthouse.

Trail Time
A full day is possible.

The St. Marks Lighthouse has stood strong on this spot through over 165 years - surviving more than 100 storms.

5

Gulf Islands National Seashore –
Naval Live Oaks

The Park

Live oak trees, prized for their rot-resistant and incredibly dense wood, have long been the lumber of choice for building durable sailing ships. Sixth President John Quincy Adams considered the United States Navy, which he called "our wooden walls," to be of critical importance in defending America from foreign invasion and in 1828 he started the country's first tree farm here for the single purpose of growing live oaks for shipbuilding.

Now a unit of the Gulf Islands National Seashore, the Naval Live Oaks area preserves 1,400 acres of forested terrain between Santa Rosa Sound and Pensacola Bay.

Santa Rosa

Phone Number
- (850) 934-2600

Website
- www.nps.gov/guis

Admission Fee
- None

Park Hours
- 8:00 a.m. to sunset

Directions
- *Gulf Breeze*; on US 98, east of town.

The Walks

There are more than seven miles of hiking trails in these historic forests. The *Brackenridge Nature Trail* is a good place to start on the south side of US 98 where exhibits identify plants and describe how live oaks were used in shipbuilding. Laid out in a figure-eight, this lush, narrow pathway runs along a bluff above the Santa Rosa Sound. You can also leave behind the casual strollers and continue down the 1.2-mile *Fishing Trail* through the thin strip of live oak forest.

Across the highway, your dog can stretch out on the sandy and wide *Andrew Jackson Trail*, a two-miler that runs the entire length of the Naval Live Oaks property. This time-worn path is a remnant of the Pensacola-St. Augustine Road, the first road connecting East Florida to West Florida. Congress ponied up $20,000 of 1824-money to build the road when Florida was still a territory.

You can use the *Jackson Trail* as a jumping off point for a full day of canine hiking on numerous side trails. Detours lead to Brown Pond and an old borrow pit from the construction of US 98.

Trail Sense: A detailed map is available from park headquarters and there are wayfinding guides on the trail.

There are always leaves on the trail under live oaks since the trees lose their leaves at different times, hence, they always appear to be "live."

Dog Friendliness
Dogs are allowed on the trails but not on the beach.
Traffic
Foot traffic only and less of it on the north side of US 98.
Canine Swimming
There are spots your dog can slip into Santa Rosa Sound for a swim.
Trail Time
Several hours to a full day.

6
Bear Creek Educational Forest

The Park

The journey of the Ochlockonee River from Georgia to the Gulf of Mexico was interrupted on the outskirts of Tallahassee in 1927 by the construction of Jackson Bluff Dam to generate electricity, create recreation and produce waterfront real estate. The river backed up enough to create the 8,850-acre Lake Talquin.

Bear Creek Educational Forest is a 492-acre tract of the Lake Talquin State Forest. Opened late in 2005, programs are offered for free to school and youth groups.

Gadsden

Phone Number
- (850) 488-1871

Website
- www.fl-dof.com/state_forests/lake_talquin.html

Admission Fee
- Vehicle parking fee

Park Hours
- Sunrise to sunset

Directions
- *Tallahassee*; west of town via I-10. Take Exit 181 and head south on SR 267 for 4.8 miles to tract entrance on left.

The Walks

The full trail system at Bear Creek sweeps away from the same trailhead as you work your way downhill to the forest's two feature routes. The *Ravine Trail* is a sporty 1.4-mile loop that travels above the vegetation-choked Beaver Pond. Your dog will be bounding up inclines and past steephead ravines as the path twists and turns.

This is the best place in Northwest Florida for tree identification. In addition to an interpretive brochure the signposts continue for the entire trip and often repeat to reinforce the learning of the native species.

More paw-friendly hiking is available on the orange-blazed *Bear Creek Trail* that traverses hardwood forests and a longleaf pine-and-wiregrass community. All the hiking at Bear Creek is under a shaded canopy and guaranteed to give your dog a workout.

Trail Sense: A park map is available and the trails well-blazed.

Bonus

The *Living Forest Trail* is a half-mile paved path that switches down the west side of a ravine.
If your dog has the patience you can stop and listen to "talking trees" describe the native trees and plants and animals by simply pushing a button.

At one time a suspension bridge swayed across Beaver Pond but today your dog will have to hike the long way around.

Dog Friendliness

Dogs are allowed on the trail but not permitted to stay in the primitive campground along the *Bear Creek Trail*.

Traffic

Foot traffic only - no horses, bikes or ATVs. You may spend your entire hike and not meet anyone for your dog to sniff.

Canine Swimming

Alligators are present in Beaver Pond.

Trail Time

More than one hour.

7
Blackwater River State Forest

The Park

Before European settlement it is believed that the slow-growing longleaf pine dominated 90 million acres of landscape from Virginia to Florida to Texas. Valued for its resin and timber, the tall, straight old growth trees - some over 300 years old - were aggressively harvested, particularly in the early 1900s. Today, less than 3% of those original longleaf pine forests remain and the greatest concentration in the world is in this part of Florida anchored by the Blackwater State Forest, Florida's largest at nearly 190,000 acres.

Reforestation of longleaf pines is an ongoing project, requiring regular burning of underbrush and aggressive hardwoods to encourage the maintenance of the fragile pine/wiregrass ecosystem.

Santa Rosa/Okaloosa

Phone Number
- (850) 957-6140

Website
- www.fl-dof.com/
state_forests/
blackwater_river.html

Admission Fee
- Parking fee in recreation areas

Park Hours
- Sunrise to sunset

Directions
(Bear Lake Recreation Area)
- *Munson*; on SR 4, 2.5 miles east of CR 191.
(Karick Lake Recreation Area)
- *Baker*; 8 miles north on CR 189.

The Walks

The vast Blackwater State Forest is not a place to bring your dog for a casual stroll; serious canine hikers only need apply. The main foot trail through the forest is the 21-mile *Jackson Red Ground Trail*; other long-distance backpacking trails include the 9-mile *Juniper Creek Trail* and the 13-mile *Wiregrass Trail*. Many segments of these pathways are part of the *Florida National Scenic Trail*.

Canine day hikers have their pick of recreation areas featuring less rigorous fare. Bear Creek is the most centrally located of these, featuring a 3.5-mile circuit hike around the 107-acre man-made lake. This narrow footpath stays above the shoreline mostly but can still be a soggy go at times. Glimpses of the lake can be had just about the entire way around.

Coming in from the west is the *Sweetwater Trail* that leads to a smaller lake in Krul Recreation Area a bit over a mile away. You can also take your dog down a two-mile connector to the *Jackson Trail* for a big day of canine hiking.

A more remote spot for day hiking in Blackwater River

Bear Lake is an ideal spot to begin your dog's exploration of the vast Blackwater River State Forest.

State Forest is Karick Lake in northwestern Okaloosa County. The trip around this 65-acre impoundment covers almost four miles, about half of the journey on the *Jackson Trail* again.

Trail Sense: The trails are blazed and trailmaps available, but from the main forest office or on the Internet, not at the trailheads.

Dog Friendliness
Dogs are permitted on the trails and in the campgrounds.

Traffic
The forest is a great place to come and be alone with your dog.

Canine Swimming
The lakes tend to have swampy shores but your dog can get in for a swim; Blackwater River forest is laced with clear water streams.

Trail Time
Several hours to an entire weekend.

29

8
Apalachicola National Forest

The Park

After a century of abuse from clear-cutting and turpentining, the land south and west of Tallahassee was riddled with runoff and scars. In 1936 the exhausted land was bundled into the Apalachicola National Forest - more than a half-million acres of low-lying cypress, longleaf pines and wiregrass savannas.

Conscientious forest management has brought back many a tree but wildlife can't always be restored. Such is the case with the red-cockaded woodpecker, a cardinal-sized, black-and-white bird with a red-streaked black hood that depends on mature pine trees for its survival. A fully grown pine tree often suffers from a fungus that makes the heartwood soft and easy to excavate for the woodpecker. Old growth pine forests have been mostly decimated and regenerated forests aren't allowed to keep their most mature trees so today the red-cockaded woodpecker has lost more than 99% of its liveable habitat. It is estimated only 15,000 birds survive today and the largest red-cockaded woodpecker population in the world lives in the Apalachicola National Forest.

several counties

Phone Number
- (850) 643-2282

Website
- www.fs.fed.us/r8/florida/recreation/index_apa.shtml

Admission Fee
- Vehicle parking fee

Park Hours
- Sunrise to sunset

Directions
- *Camel Lake*; CR 105 west off SR 65.
Wright Lake; CR 101 west off SR 65.

The Walks

About 69 of the 85 miles of trails here come on the long-distance *Florida National Scenic Trail* but canine day hikers will want to focus on the loops at Wright Lake and Camel Lake. The *Wright Lake Loop* mixes cypress and wetlands into its five miles, using wooden bridges to ferry across numerous creeks. This is an easy, shady two-hour ramble for your dog.

More challenging is the nine-mile *Trail of the Lakes* that combines with the orange-blazed *Florida Trail* to close the loop. You can warm up for this rollicking canine hike with a tour of the one-mile *Camel Lake Interpretive Trail*.

For a real challenge in the Apalachicola National Forest there is the 13-mile stretch of the Florida Trail that routes directly through the notorious Bradwell Bay Wilderness Area. At full strength, this passage requires sloshing through waist-high water that has led *Backpacking Magazine* to call it one of the toughest hikes in America. Certainly no place for a dog but in times of drought it is well worth checking out for its eerie beauty.

Trail Sense: There are wayfinding aids in abundance from informational kiosks to signage to energetic trail blazing.

Dog Friendliness
Dogs are permitted on the trails and in the recreation areas.
Traffic
There are trails for equestrians, trails for off-road vehicles, trails for bikes and trails for hikers.
Canine Swimming
Alligators and snakes are ever-present but there are plenty of places for your dog to slip into the water.
Trail Time
Several hours to a week.

9
Florida Caverns State Park

The Park

It has only been the blink of an eye, geologically speaking, that Florida has not been under water. During its time undersea, coral, shellfish, and fish skeletons piled up. This created a layer of limestone hundreds of feet thick. When the sea level fell, acidic groundwater gradually dissolved the porous limestone to form cracks and passages. In this part of the Florida panhandle the rock has been pushed up and there are some sizable hills. This area includes numerous caves.

The highly decorated Florida Cavern is as ornate as many of the celebrated tourist caves around the country. Altogether, there are 10 acres of caves here. During the Seminole Wars, they were used as hideouts. In the 1930s, the Civilian Conservation Corp developed the cave for visitors, removing mud, widening passages, and excavating where necessary to provide headroom.

The Walks

Has your Northwest Florida dog ever seen a rock? Well he certainly can here. The delightful *Visitor Center Trail*

Jackson

Phone Number
- (850) 482-9598

Website
- www.floridastateparks.org/floridacaverns

Admission Fee
- Entrance fee required

Park Hours
- 8:00 a.m. to sunset

Directions
- *Marianna*; 3 miles north of town on SR 166. Use Exit 136 or Exit 142 off I-10 to reach Marianna.

Florida Caverns may be the only place your dog will hike in Northwest Florida and see a rock.

Bonus

Your dog is not allowed to tour Florida Cavern but he can find his own unique underground adventure on the trail in Tunnel Cave.

It isn't Florida Cavern but for 100 feet your dog will travel underground on the **Visitor Center Trail.**

Trail is the only trail in the panhandle that winds through rocky terrain - a fairy garden of whimsical limestone formations. The towering hardwoods frame the trail as it visits twenty-foot vertical bluffs above the floodplain and descends down to swampland where tupelo gums are anchored in the soggy soil. Be careful of your footing where leaves have obscured the path.

For longer, albeit more traditional Florida hiking fare, head up to the multi-use *Upper Chipola Trails* that explore the basin of the Chipola River. The waterway collects water from 63 springs, the largest number of any rivershed in Northwest Florida. There are more than six miles of shaded woodland trails across the rolling terrain here.

Trail Sense: The trails are signed and trailmaps lead the way.

Dog Friendliness

Dogs are not allowed in the cave or in the swimming facility at Blue Hole Spring but can hike the trails.

Traffic

Foot traffic only around the Visitor Center but horses and bikes can use the expansive trail system in the northwest region of the park.

Canine Swimming

Your dog can find his way into the Chipola River but it is hardly a swimming dog's paradise.

10
Pine Log
State Forest

The Park

Pine Log is Florida's first state forest, purchased in 1936. The nearly 7,000 acres are managed for a variety of uses including timber production (over $1 million worth of lumber has been harvested in the past 20 years), wildlife preservation and outdoor recreation.

The Walks

For a pure get-out-in-the-woods-and-hike-with-your-dog outing, it is hard to top Pine Log State Forest. The Division of Forestry has carved three trail systems through the slash and longleaf pine forests.

Bay/Washington

Phone Number
- (850) 535-2888

Website
- www.fl-dof.com/
state_forests/pine_log.html

Admission Fee
- Parking fee for day use

Park Hours
- Sunrise to sunset

Directions
- *Ebro*; from US 20 the trailheads are south of town along SR 79.

The *Old Sawmill Trail* was developed for horses and the *Crooked Creek Trail* built for off-road bikes and while these long distance trails are open to your dog as well, most canine hikers will want to head to the Sand Pond Recreation Area first.

The marquis loop at Sand Pond is the 5.5-mile, blue-blazed *Dutch & Faye Trail*, named for Edgar "Dutch" Tiemann and his wife. Tiemann was the first park ranger assigned to Pine Log State Forest in 1978 and he laid out most of the routes down to Pine Log Creek and back. The trail, sometimes narrow as it picks through the pines, benefits from a rolling terrain and plenty of twists that will keep you dog wondering what's around the next bend.

If you don't want to sign on for the entire two-hour tour you can detour onto the orange-blazed *Florida National Scenic Trail*. The Florida Trail is developed for eight miles across the forest. Also available at Sand Pond is the easy-going *Campground Boardwalk Trail* that can be completed by even an inexperienced trail dog in less than one hour.

Trail Sense: Trailmaps are available at the the trailhead and the routes are well-blazed, although trail crossings will give moment for pause.

34

It's not all pine trees in the Pine Log State Forest as your dog will discover when exploring the cypress swamp.

Dog Friendliness
Dogs are allowed on the trails and in the campground.

Traffic
The Tiemann trail is open to bikes as well as foot traffic. Foot traffic only on the *Boardwalk Trail* but you can go for hours and never see another trail user on any of the Pine Log State Forest systems.

Canine Swimming
Sand Pond at the campground is an ideal doggie swimming hole.

Trail Time
Several hours to a full day.

II
Camp Helen
State Park

The Park

Surrounded by water on three sides, the advantageous positioning of this peninsula on the Gulf of Mexico has long attracted human settlement. Shell middens found here have been traced back 4000 years.

In 1928, Robert E. Hicks acquired 185 acres along Lake Powell to create a summer retreat for his wife Margret May who named the compound Loch Lomond. Following World War II, Avondale Mills of Sylacauaga, Alabama purchased the property as a resort for its vacationing textile workers.

They operated Camp Helen, named for the founder's daughter-in-law, for 39 years, building utilitarian cottages and an opulent log lodge that still stand in the park. The State of Florida acquired the land in 1994.

Bay
Phone Number - (850) 233-5059
Website - www.floridastateparks.org/camphelen
Admission Fee - Yes, a parking fee
Park Hours - 8:00 a.m to sunset
Directions - *Panama City Beach*; at the west terminus of the Lake Powell Bridge on US 98, 12 miles east of SR 331 or 7 miles west of SR 79.

The Walks

It is easy to blow past Camp Helen when traveling along US 98 and that would be a loss for your trail-loving dog. There is only one trail in the park, covering a bit over one mile, but it is sure to be one of your dog's favorites.

After exploring the lodge and cottages of Camp Helen the trail drops to the shores of Lake Powell, one of Florida's largest examples of a rare coastal dune lake. At several spots your dog can slip into the water for a cooling dip. Moving on you soon traverse a salt marsh before bursting onto the wide, sugary sands of the Gulf of Mexico. Although your dog can't continue all the way to the Inlet Beach proper, this is one of the few places he can trot the sands, see the waves and at least feel like it's a day at the beach.

Before your dog can get too giddy, however, the trail turns up into the dunes and shortly you reach a dense maritime hammock and the shade of moss-draped live oaks and tall pines. The wide, sandy path swings past Duck Pond before finishing back among the camp buildings of the old resort. All in all, quite a bit to pique your dog's interest here.

Trail Sense: A trailmap and signs will get you where you want to go.

At Camp Helen, your dog can feel like he's on a Gulf of Mexico beach - even if he can't quite get there.

Dog Friendliness
Dogs are welcome on the trails but not on the beach.
Traffic
Foot traffic only in this peaceful park.
Canine Swimming
Alligators are present in the park but there is access to Lake Powell.
Trail Time
An hour or more is possible.

12
Elinor Klapp-
Phipps Park

The Park

The land for this 509-acre park was first cultivated in the 1800s as a medium-sized cotton plantation known as Mossview. In 1915 the property was developed by Arthur Lapsley as a quail hunting retreat and rechristened Meridian Plantation.

In 1933, Meridian Plantation was purchased by Dwight F. Davis who had served as Secretary of War in President Herbert Hoover's cabinet and was just finishing up a stint as Governor General of the Phillipines. Davis lived at Meridian until his death in 1945.

The property was acquired by Griscom Bettle followed by John H. Phipps and in 1958 inherited by Colin Phipps. The City of Tallahassee purchased land here to preserve and protect the water quality of Lake Jackson.

Leon

Phone Number
- (850) 539-5999

Website
- None

Admission Fee
- None

Park Hours
- Sunrise to sunset

Directions
- *Tallahassee*; take Exit 203 off I-10 onto Route 61 north. Make the first left on Maclay Avenue and follow to the end. Turn right on Meridian Road and the park entrances are on the left. Use the first entrance, the recreation/ballfields. Another trailhead can be reached by continuing north on Meridian and turning left on Miller Landing Road. This trailhead is recommended for longer outings on the trail.

The Walks

The woodlands of Elinor Klapp-Phipps Park are laced with miles of trails - more than ten for bikes and horses and seven for foot traffic only. One of the delights in bringing your dog here is the dips and rolls in topography; nothing dramatic but enough elevation change for diverse ecosystems to flourish.

Canine hikers have their choice of two trail loops, each around two miles in length. The *Swamp Forest Loop* brings more of the Florida hills into play while the *Coonbottom Loop* follows just about every twist and turn in the sand-bottom stream. The trails can be tight in spots and keep your dog high-stepping to avoid roots obscured by leaf litter on the soft dirt paths. If your dog is a fan of butterflies, head out to the *Swamp Forest Loop* and pick up an identification brochure.

If your dog wants more here a connector trail (almost one mile) leads out to the 2.5-mile *Oak Hammock Loop* that trips along the shores of Lake Jackson.

The sand-bottom stream is the dominant feature of the serpentine **Coonbottom Loop.**

Trail Sense: This is the best marked park in Northwest Florida - the routes are energetically blazed, mapboards are posted at the trailheads and the mailboxes at the trailheads may even be stocked with brochures. Distance signs are also posted at trail junctions.

Dog Friendliness
Dogs are allowed to hike these trails.
Traffic
No bikes or horses are permitted on the hiking trails and you may go a long time without seeing other hikers, many of whom seem to prefer the roomier Lake Overstreet Trails across the street.
Canine Swimming
The streams that percolate across the property provide a refreshing break at best; dogs are not allowed to swim in Lake Jackson.
Trail Time
More than one hour.

13

Grayton Beach State Park

The Park

When Colonel Charles T. Gray built a small home here in 1885, the windswept dunes were a lonely place. There were no roads or bridges to get there and if you did come to settle you couldn't grow anything in the sandy soil. There wasn't another settlement around for another five miles until 1890 when more military men arrived and named one of Walton county's beach communities after Gray.

When US 98 was built in the 1930s Grayton Beach became less remote but electricity still didn't arrive until the 1940s. The State of Florida began buying land at Grayton in 1964 through a lease from the Florida Board of Education and opened the state park in 1968. In 1985, after years of lobbying by residents, Florida bought the village's beach front and the dunes and forest land to the west and north, virtually surrounding the village of Grayton Beach with more than 2,000 acres of parkland.

Walton
Phone Number - (850) 231-4210
Website - www.floridastateparks.org/graytonbeach
Admission Fee - Vehicle entrance fee
Park Hours - 8:00 a.m. to sunset
Directions - *Santa Rosa Beach*; on CR 30A, south of US 98 and east of CR 283.

The Walks

The star hike for your dog at Grayton Beach is the nature trail that is squeezed in the wild dunesland between the Gulf of Mexico and Western Lake. You will find this double loop at the very end of the paved parking lot. Your dog will be ushered into the *Barrier Dunes Trail* through a tunnel of scrub oak twisted by the Gulf breezes and salt spray. Although separated from the sunbathers enjoying one of America's perenially top-rated beaches by only a few yards, you are a world away.

The sand trail emerges on the shores of Western Lake where it joins the *Pine Woods Loop* and a totally different natural community on the backside

40

of the dunes. Sand gives way to a wooden boardwalk for part of the trip. The tall, slender pines afford a measure of shade on the shifting sands.

For more conventional canine hiking, the *Grayton Beach Hike/Bike Trail* explores more than 1000 undeveloped acres on the north side of Route 30A. There is only limited parking off the side of the road at the trailhead, however, so you may need to add a couple round-trip miles of hiking to reach this 4.5-mile trail system.

Scrub oak sculpted by the wind form a cave-like entrance to the **Barrier Dunes Trail.**

Trail Sense: A park map locates the trailhead and trail signs keep you moving in the right direction.

Dog Friendliness
Dogs are welcome on the trails, in the campground and at the picnic areas but not on the beach or in the cabins.
Traffic
Most folks are coming for the sparkling beach but the trail users you find on the nature trails will only be on foot.
Canine Swimming
There is access to Western Lake on the trails.
Trail Time
More than one hour.

14
Tate's Hell
State Forest

The Park

Cebe Tate's "hell" was a week he spent lost in a swamp in 1875 tracking a panther that was killing his livestock. He was bitten by a snake and forced to drink rancid water. Finally he burst into a clearing near Carrabelle, living only long enough to murmur the words, "My name is Cebe Tate, and I just came from Hell!" At least he had his hunting dogs with him at the end.

No one much bothered with Tate's Hell for 100 years after that until the timber industry drastically altered the hydrology of the swamp to establish pine plantations in the 1960s. In the 1990s, with the Apalachicola Bay being threatened with severe freshwater run-off, the state of Florida began purchasing land here and now has over 100,000 acres under protection and natural restoration.

Franklin

Phone Number
- (850) 697-3734

Website
- www.fl-dof.com/
state_forests/tates_hell.html

Admission Fee
- None

Park Hours
- Sunrise to sunset

Directions
- *Carrabelle*; there are two parking lots on the north side of US 98 at each terminus of the *High Bluff Coastal Hiking Trail*, one just west of Carrabelle and the other east of Eastpoint.

The Walks

Your dog is likely to figure he is closer to heaven than hell when hiking here. Tate's Hell State Forest has only one dedicated hiking trail but it is a beauty. The *High Bluff Coastal Hiking Trail* is a linear 4-mile, natural surface pathway through a coastal scrub habitat. The ancient sand dunes have been colonized by small oaks, saw palmetto and isolated groups of sand pines that let plenty of sunlight in along the trail. When the route drops off the ridge, the scrub gives way to shady pines.

Under paw your dog will enjoy a soft sand and pine straw surface along the roomy path. Up above, eagles and osprey soar and a Florida black bear may even stray this far down to the coast.

Hiking on the **High Bluff Coastal Trail** *is anything but a hell for your dog.*

Trail Sense: Trailmaps are available at the trailhead and there are blazes and mile markers to keep you from heading down a stray jeep road.

Dog Friendliness
Dogs are permitted on the *High Bluff Coastal Hiking Trail*.
Traffic
Foot traffic only and not a great deal of it.
Canine Swimming
None, but down the road in Carrabelle Beach is one of the few places you can take your dog to the beach along the Gulf of Mexico. Pull off the road at a rest stop on the ocean side of US 98.
Trail Time
More than one hour.

43

J.R. Alford Greenway

The Park

Lake Lafayette was originally considered a prairie lake since it took on the appearance of a grasslaand during periods of drought. A magnet for early settlement, almost 40 Indian mounds have been identified in the Lafayette Basin.

The lake takes it name from the Marquis de Lafayette, who was granted a 36 square-mile tract in 1824 for his military service during the American Revolution a half-century earlier.

Large tracts were soon sold off for cotton plantations. Here, on the north side of the lake, Francis Epps, a grandson of Thomas Jefferson, and Green Chaires from Jacksonville became the dominant planters. During the 2nd Seminole War of 1835-1842, Chaires' wife, two of his children and several slaves were murdered and the family mansion destroyed.

In the late 1940s dikes were constructed that turned the central part of the lake into a farm pond and created the Alford Arm. This 874-acre swath of open space was acquired in 2001 as a Trust of Public Land Project.

Leon
Phone Number - None
Website - www.leoncountyfl.gov/parks/greenways.asp
Admission Fee - None
Park Hours - Sunrise to sunset
Directions - *Tallahassee*; from I-10 take Exit 203 south on US 319. Turn left on US 90 and after a half-mile turn right on Buck Lake Road. Make a right on Pedrick Road to the parking area.

The Walks

This is the Godzilla of local area hiking with nearly 20 miles of trails available. Bounding from the car, your dog is greeted by a sloping grass field of 60 acres that begs to be romped across. This is the best open-air hiking in Northwest Florida. The main clay road-trail trips away from the parking lot to the wooded, primitive trails in the distance.

There are four designated trail designations for bikes, horses and foot traffic so you can direct your dog to the routes where only feet and paws are permitted.

Wherever you go, however, don't come with a time constraint. This is a place for long, leisurely canine hikes. Or maybe just to sit out in the middle of the field with your dog on a sunny day.

Trail Sense: Maps posted at the trailhead kiosks will get you pointed in the right direction and there is a map that can be printed off the Internet - and it will come in handy.

Dog Friendliness
Dogs are allowed to hike these trails and poop bags are provided.

Traffic
No motorized vehicles are allowed and there are trails dedicated to equestrians and bike riders. Also a popular spot for cross-country runners.

Canine Swimming
Bring your dog's water here.

Trail Time
Several hours to a full day.

Let's get started! Wide open spaces beckon at Alford Greenway.

45

16

Falling Waters
State Park

The Park

At 73 feet, Falling Waters is home to Florida's tallest waterfall. The potential of power generated from tumbling water disappearing into a cave at the bottom of a sinkhole attracted industry in the 19th century. A grist mill operated here, grinding corn into grits and cornmeal during the Civil War. After it was abandoned, timbers - some on display in the park - fell into Falling Waters Sink.

In 1891, a whiskey distillery just above the waterfall provided legal hooch for nearby railway workers. When the still went away the Glen St. Mary Nursery operated here but it failed during the Depression of the 1930s, leaving behind exotic species such as mimosa, Japanese privet and date palm on the property.

Washington

Phone Number
- (850) 638-6130

Website
- www.floridastateparks.org/fallingwaters

Admission Fee
- Vehicle entrance fee

Park Hours
- 8:00 a.m. to sunset

Directions
- *Chipley*; three miles south of town. Take Exit 120 off I-10 and go south on SR 77 for one mile. Turn left on State Park Road and follow to the entrance.

The Walks

At Falling Waters you take your dog into woods of towering Southern pines and Northern hardwoods but it doesn't take long for this hike to cease to resemble a typical forest walk. In short order you are introduced to fern-draped sinkholes, the namesake waterfall, a wiregrass prairie, and a two-acre lake.

The trail system essentially links the *Sinks Trail* to the *Wiregrass Trail* to the *Terrace Trail*. Starting from the parking lot your dog will be working up one of Flordia's highest hills to an elevation of 324 feet in the campground. Probably not enough to set him to panting but midway the trail passes by the lake where your dog can slip in for a quick refresher. Detailed plant identification brochures accompany the trail to explain the rich biodiversity that exists along the Branch Creek. Your dog will be trotting on elaborate boardwalks and the remnants of old country roads.

Trail Sense: A park map keeps you oriented comfortably.

Dog Friendliness
Dogs are allowed on the trail and in the campground but not on the beach at the lake.

Traffic
Foot traffic only; the boardwalks can get crowded in season.

Canine Swimming
Your dog can put a paw in the park lake away from the beach.

Trail Time
About one hour.

Most of Florida's highest waterfall falls underground.

17
Fort Braden Trails

The Park

During the Second Seminole War a garrison was established on the Ochlockonee River on December 3, 1839. The fort was the site of some skirmishing but was otherwise abandoned on June 7, 1842 at war's end without notoriety.

In its short existence, however, a small community sprouted to support the fort and it has carried the name into the 21st century. The Fort Braden Tract is a day-use area developed in the Lake Talquin State Forest on the lake's south shore.

Leon

Phone Number
- (850) 488-1871

Website
- www.fl-dof.com/state_forests/lake_talquin.html

Admission Fee
- Vehicle parking fee

Park Hours
- Sunrise to sunset

Directions
- *Tallahassee*; go west 8.7 miles on SR 20 from Capital Circle, SR 263. Entrance is on the right.

The Walks

As you take your dog down the broad entrance road from the parking lot, the woods that spread before you seem to be one identical canvas. The Fort Braden Trails, in fact, consist of three separate loops, each about three miles in length, with their own distinct character.

The *East Loop* has the most elevation changes of all the trails, dipping into small stream-cut ravines angling towards Lake Talquin. The *Center Loop* features the tract's largest hardwood forest and is crisscrossed by seepage streams. There is enough slope on the property that these waterways can host tiny waterfalls. The *West Loop* mixes thick stands of pines into the hardwoods and the trail is at times blanketed in handfuls of pine needles rather than leaf cover on the other trails.

While trotting your dog will often be picking her way along narrow ribbons through the light airy woods but will never feel hemmed in. The little rolls in terrain add character to the hike. Look for tree roots and cuppy going when you have to share the trail with horses.

Trail Sense: The routes are well-blazed but there are times when the hiking and equestrian trails merge or cross so pay attention and keep your dog's nose pointed in the right direction. Take a moment to study the entrance to the woods - the trailhead signs are tucked back into the trees and not easily spotted.

Dog Friendliness
Dogs are permitted across all trails.

Traffic
No bikes are allowed on the trails and you can expect long stretches of solitude with your dog at Fort Braden.

Canine Swimming
The waters of Lake Talquin are not easily accessed from the shore that is situated a few feet above the waterline.

Trail Time
More than one hour.

18
Miccosukee Canopy Road Greenway

The Park

These rolling hills were originally cleared by cotton planters in the 1800s. As the soil tuckered out, the plantations failed and wealthy northerners seeking warm-weather retreats came around with checks in hand. Udo Fleischmann, heir to the fortune created by the development of America's first commerical yeast and scion of New Jersey horse country, began purchasing property here in 1912, building a 7,000-acre quail hunting plantation he called Welaunee.

After his death in 1952, Udo Fleischmann left the estate to his wife who raised prized Hereford cattle in this quiet corner of Northwest Florida.

With development pressures, a large chunk of the Welaunee Plantation has been carefully preserved since 1998 in the Miccosukee Greenway by the Trust for Public Land, Leon County and private owners. In 2007 the trail was designated a National Recreation Trail.

Leon
Phone Number - (850) 488-0221
Website - www.dep.state.fl.us/gwt/ guide/regions/panhandleeast/ trails/miccosukee_canopy_ rd.htm
Admission Fee - None
Park Hours - Sunrise to sunset
Directions - *Tallahassee*; from I-10, take Exit 209 west. Turn right on Edenfield Road to Miccosukee Road; parking is on the north side of the road.

The Walks

The Miccosukee Canopy Road Greenway packs more than a dozen miles of trail into a 503-acre linear park stuffed between the roadway and a boundary fence. The main parking lot is roughly at the center of a six-mile stretch of Miccosukee Road. The primary trail, wide and paw-friendly, more or less loops in both directions.

The greatest joy of hiking with your dog along the Miccosukee Greenway is the rolling hills and open vistas of pastureland that are rare in Northwest

Florida. Your dog may even chance to see a cow or two. To emphasize the laid-back feel of an outing at Miccosukee benches are interspersed along the trails.

Trail Sense: A park map is available but you can explore without it; there are off-shoots of the main trail throughout but you won't need a rescue dog in this narrow slice of parkland.

Dog Friendliness
Dogs are welcome on the Greenway.

Traffic
Runners and bikers favor Miccosukee Road - and be on the alert for a stray cross-country team.

Canine Swimming
Not enough water to quench a swimming dog's thirst.

Trail Time
More than one hour.

When a live oak is given the chance to grow in open spaces they can grow to enormous size, like the ones decorating Miccosukee Road.

19
Point Washington State Forest

The Park

Point Washington State Forest was purchased under Florida's Conservation and Recreation Lands Program in 1992. The area had been extensively logged and under the stewardship of the Department of Agriculture and Consumer Services, the Division of Forestry has planted more than one million longleaf pines.

While juggling timber management, wildlife management and ecological restoration across 15,000 acres the state has developed the *Eastern Lake Trail System* for outdoor enthusiasts.

Walton

Phone Number
- (850) 231-5800

Website
- www.fl-dof.com/
state_forests/
point_washington.html

Admission Fee
- Entrance fee required

Park Hours
- Sunrise to sunset

Directions
- *Freeport*; 9 miles south
of US 98 on CR 395.

The Walks

The primary hiking through Point Washington State Forest is a ten-mile, orange blazed loop with two cut-off road/trails that give you options of three-mile and five-mile trips with your dog. Most of the trail is laid across wide double-track and jeep roads. The surface under paw ranges from thick sugar sand to easier going on packed sand jeep roads.

As you mosey along you'll visit coastal pine scrub and cypress swamps and duck under leafy canopies but most of your canine hiking in the forest will be through regenerating pine flatwoods. The trees are still only 20 to 30 feet tall in most places so there is plenty of sunlight that warms the trail under the open sky. This is almost universally flat going for your dog.

Trail Sense: A trailmap is available at the trailhead; the routes are blazed, mile markers are posted along the way and information kiosks are placed at key trail junctions. Still, be careful of the intrusion of old woods roads.

Dog Friendliness
Dogs are allowed across the *Eastern Lake Trail System*.

Traffic
Motorized vehicles are not allowed but bikes will share the trails. Still, do not expect much competition for these trails.

Canine Swimming
Come to trot, not to swim.

Trail Time
Loops of one, two or three hours are available.

The Division of Foresty has been busy in Point Washington State Forest. This is the one-millionth tree planted in the forest.

20
Wakulla Springs State Park

The Park

Legend has it that when Spanish explorer Ponce de Leon claimed to have discovered his "fountain of youth" in 1513, it was Wakulla Springs that he was sampling. One of the world's largest and deepest freshwater springs, the bowl of the main spring spreads across three acres and pumps thousands of gallons of steady 68-degree water per second. On April 11, 1973 peak flow was measured at the rate of 1.2 billion gallons per day!

So crystal clear are the waters that your dog can spot a meatbone 185 feet down on the bottom. The source of Wakulla Springs remains a mystery. An extensive underwater cave system has been explored to a depth of 300 feet and mapped for more than a mile without revealing the tap of the great flow.

Designated a National Natural Landmark in 1966, Wakulla Springs became a state park 20 years later and today is a 6,000-acre wildlife sanctuary.

Wakulla

Phone Number
- (850) 224-5950

Website
- http://www.floridastateparks.org/wakullasprings

Admission Fee
- Yes

Park Hours
- Sunrise to sunset

Directions
- *Wakulla Springs*; from Tallahassee go 16 miles south on SR 61. Turn left on SR 267 and the entrance is immediately on the right.

The Walks

Your dog won't be able to experience the mystical Wakulla waters - dogs are not allowed beyond a chain link fence that lines the shore. The fence was actually erected by landowner Edward Ball more than fifty years ago to keep boaters away from the springs. He was sued for fencing a navigable waterway but Ball won and the fence survives, as does the opulent Mediterrean Revival style Wakulla Lodge.

Still, there is plenty of interest for the canine hiker in Wakulla Springs State Park. Two trails - the *Short Trail* and *Long Trail* - combine for a total of almost

three canopied miles through pine and hardwood forests, cypress swamps, and floodplain basins. Surrounded by indigenous Florida plants, the trails are wide and soft under paw and universally flat.

Trail Sense: The trails wrap around the entrance road, never straying far enough away to require the park map.

Dog Friendliness

Dogs are not allowed in the springs area.

Traffic

A multi-use trail courses across the northern tier of the park but the nature trails are reserved for foot traffic only.

Canine Swimming

None, there are alligators in the Wakulla River.

Trail Time

About an hour.

21

Ochlockonee River State Park

The Park

In 1998 a shell midden identified on the banks of the Dead River traced human habitation here back 1500 years. The land, owned by the federal government, was widely tapped over the decades for its pine resin.

On May 14, 1970 the State of Florida acquired the slab of land at the confluence of the Dead and Ochlockonee (meaning "yellow") rivers that would become the park in a land exchange.

The Walks

Blessed by two scenic rivers, this is a popular destination for water recreation - and the quiet trails will keep your dog's tail wagging as well. Upon passing through the park tollgate follow the road to the Tide Creek Picnic Shelter where the waters of the Dead River and Ochockonee River mingle. This is the departure point for two nature trails.

The *River Nature Trail* picks its way along the banks of the Ochlockonee on a narrow, sandy path above the water. Every now and then a sliver of sand beach appears where your dog can bound down and sample the mix of fresh and brackish waters. This out-and-back excursion will cover the better part of 1.5 miles, or you can take a spur trail through the campground to the...

...*Pine Flatwoods Trail*. This prototypical Florida hiking trail travels across pinelands rigorously maintained through prescribed burning. In this heart of the park is Florida's most significant concentration of the endangered red-cockaded woodpecker. Nesting in cavities of tall, straight pines, the birds are critical to the health of Florida's signature pineland/wiregrass community.

Trail Sense: A trailmap is available and signs keep you oriented.

Wakulla

Phone Number
- (850) 962-2771

Website
- www.floridastateparks.org/ochlockoneeriver

Admission Fee
- Yes, a vehicle entrance fee

Park Hours
- 8:00 a.m to sunset

Directions
- *Sopchoppy*; on US 319, four miles south of town, between SR 375 and US 98.

Ochlockonee River is home to a population of white squirrels. These curious creatures are not albinos but are pigmentally-challenged gray squirrels carrying a gene mutation. Brevard, North Carolina is the acknowledged capital of white squirrels in the United States but theirs were originally imports from Florida. How did they come to Northwest Florida? Legend has it that a Chinese princess traveling aboard ship up the Ochlockonee River lost her pair of pet white squirrels who happily began breeding once they reached shore.

Dog Friendliness
Dogs are allowed on the trails and in the campground.

Traffic
Foot traffic only; the *River Nature Trail* can become a communal hike as it passes close by campsites, the boat launch and fishing holes.

Canine Swimming
Alligators are present which negates unfettered dog paddling in the inviting rivers.

Trail Time
An hour or more is possible.

The serene waters of the Ochlockonee River are ideally suited for all sorts of activity.

22
Alfred B. Maclay Gardens State Park

The Park

In 1923, Alfred Maclay, a prosperous New York money man, came to Tallahassee's Red Hills and bought a winter home on the shores of Lake Hall. He named his new family retreat *Killearn Plantation and Gardens* after his ancestral home in Scotland.

An enthusiastic gardener, Maclay quickly set about planting camellias, azaleas, magnolias and other ornamentals under the towering pines and spreading live oaks that had thrived on the property for decades. The beauty of his gardens gained national acclaim.

Maclay died in 1944 and nine years later his wife, Louise, donated the gardens to the state. Most importantly for dog owners, the State of Florida acquired over 1000 acres of pristine woodlands around the adjoining Lake Overstreet in 1994.

Leon

Phone Number
- (850) 487-4556

Website
- www.floridastateparks.org/ maclaygardens

Admission Fee
- There is a vehicle parking fee at the main entrance; you can also park at Elinor Klapp-Phipps Park on Meridian Road, walk to the *Overstreet Trails* and pay a dollar trail user fee

Park Hours
- Sunrise to sunset at Overstreet; 8:00 a.m to sunset through the main entrance

Directions
- *Tallahassee*; take I-10 to Exit 203 and go north. Turn left onto Maclay Road and stay in the right lane for the park.

The Walks

Canine hikers have a choice of how to attack the *Overstreet Trail* system in this beautiful park. For dogs looking for a modest outing of less than an hour, choose the *Ravine Trail*, best accessed from Elinor Klapp-Phipps Park. Here, the loop, almost universally level and traversed on wide, hard-packed, paw-friendly trails, covers a bit less than two miles.

The star walk at Maclay Gardens is the circumnavigation of the secluded Lake Overstreet. Once you start out on this journey you sign on for the entire three-mile trip. The *Lake Trail* can be reached from either the parking lot in the gardens or the lot on Meridian Street. Aside from open air hiking down a power cut, the going is almost universally shaded for your dog here. There are views of the lake and down adjoining ravines as you pass.

Trail Sense: A trail map is available and a mapboard to study. The trail system is simply laid out which is good since there are no markings.

Dog Friendliness

Dogs are allowed on the *Overstreet Trails* but can not go into the formal gardens.

Traffic

Bikes and horses are allowed on these multi-use trails.

Canine Swimming

Lake Overstreet and Gum Pond are not choice swimming holes except for the most determined of water-loving dogs.

Trail Time

Several hours possible.

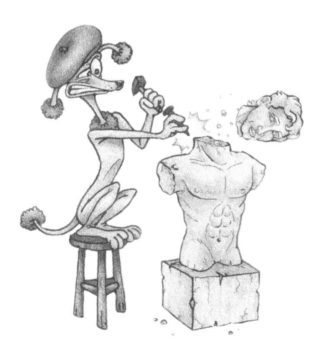

23
St. George Island State Park

The Park

From studying middens, or trash mounds, anthropologists believe St. George Island, a natural barrier island, was first inhabited by the Creek Indians between the 900s and 1400s. In 1803, the Creek Indians ceded a large tract of land, which included St. George Island, to trader John Forbes and Company, known as the Forbes Grant. Thereafter, visitors from the mainland mainly sailed over to collect oysters and shellfish.

In the 20th century the island's pine forest was energetically exploited for turpentine production. In 1965 the Bryant G. Patton Bridge was completed from Eastpoint across Apalachicola Bay, opening St. George Island to increased recreational use. The state of Florida had already begun acquiring parkland and in 1980 the state park officially opened with nearly 2,000 acres protected at the island's eastern tip.

Franklin

Phone Number
- (850) 927-2111

Website
- www.floridastateparks.org/stgeorgeisland

Admission Fee
- A vehicle entrance fee

Park Hours
- 8:00 a.m to sunset

Directions
- *St. George Island*; from US 98 in Eastpoint take the Patton Bridge to the island and turn left at the light, following CR 300, to the park entrance.

The Walks

If you ever want to get the feeling you are walking to the end of the world with your dog, St. George is a good place to come. Beyond the gate where the pavement ends, you start hiking to the the east end of the island. Along the way you'll pass through salt marshes, dunes covered in sea oats and stands of pines. A round trip can last many hours.

Trail Sense: None needed.

In September 1941 the United States Army opened Camp Carrabelle, later to be named Camp Gordon Johnston, in honor of a colonel who served in three wars and earned many decorations including the Congressional Medal of Honor for bravery during the Philippine Insurrection in 1906.

Camp Gordon Johnston covered 165,000 acres and extended 36 miles along the Gulf of Mexico. Utilizing Florida's sandy beaches, swamps, and jungle-like forests, the installation was an amphibious training camp, providing some of the toughest military training in the world. St. George Island, uninhabited at that time, was used to practice invasions and amphibious landings. The camp was deactivated and closed in 1946.

Dog Friendliness

Dogs are allowed on the trails and in the campground but not on the beach or in the primitive campsites or in the picnic pavillions.

Traffic

Bikes are allowed on the road but most of the island can only be explored by foot; come in the off-season and you may never see anyone.

Canine Swimming

You can find spots along St. George Sound where the water does not equal the beach.

Trail Time

Several hours possible.

24
Tarkiln Bayou State Park

The Park

The Perdido River was named by the Spanish who occupied the area until 1813. The word "perdido" in Spanish is translated as "lost." Before this unusual wet prairie habitat was indeed lost, a Florida Forever purchase protected the Perdido Pitcher Plant Prairie on the banks of the bay.

This is one of the largest stands of the rare white-top pitcher plant in Florida. The insect-feeding stalk is unique to the Gulf Coast and found only between the Apalachicola and Mississippi Rivers. Almost 100 other rare plants and animals depend on the unusual wet prairie habitat, including the alligator snapping turtle, sweet pitcher plant and Chapman's butterwort.

Since the original acquisition in 1998, the Perdido Pitcher Plant Prairie, now the Tarkiln Bayou State Park, has continued to add chunks of protected land.

Escambia

Phone Number
- None

Website
- www.floridastateparks.org/tarkilnbayou

Admission Fee
- None

Park Hours
- 8:00 a.m to sunset

Directions
- *Pensacola*; from US 98 take CR 293 south to to the gravel parking area on the right.

The Walks

There are two trails available, both completely under the canopy of airy pine flatlands. Bearing left, is the shorter of the two, a handicap accessible sidewalk that eventually gives way to a long boardwalk that crosses prime pitcher plant habitat before bursting out on the bayou in a half-mile. An old sandy-dirt road parallels the sidewalk until the boardwalk if you don't need to wear your dog's nails down on the concrete.

The longer option drifts to the right on its way to the bay on a natural, sometimes narrow surface. This is the path that leads into the teeth of the wet prairie although you can discover signature pitcher plants anywhere across the Preserve.

Trail Sense: No help here, save for a rudimentary map on the information board at the trailhead but it is difficult to get lost.

Dog Friendliness
  Dogs are allowed on these trails.

Traffic
  Foot traffic only and little of it in this peaceful park.

Canine Swimming
  None.

Trail Time
  More than one hour.

25
Bald Point State Park

The Park

The St. Joe Company traces its beginnings to the 1920s when Alfred I. duPont arrived in Florida after fleeing his meddling relatives in the family chemical business. With a dream of starting a paper company, duPont began spending his millions on undeveloped Northwest Florida real estate. His acquisitions were added to the balance sheet in chunks of hundreds of thousands of acres.

Alfred died in 1935 before realizing his dream but his brother-in-law, Edward Ball, organized the St. Joe Paper Company with his assets. Today the Company owns approximately 838,000 acres, 338,000 of which are within ten miles of the Gulf of Mexico, including Alligator Point.

Facing developmental pressure, the privately-funded Trust for Public Land was responsible for the transfer of ownership of 1,348 acres of Bald Point, historically used as an informal open space, to the State of Florida. Later, the Nature Conservancy negotiated to receive an additional 2,851 donated acres from the St. Joe Company.

Franklin

Phone Number
- (850) 349-9146

Website
- www.floridastateparks.org/baldpoint

Admission Fee
- Parking fee required

Park Hours
- 8:00 a.m. to 8:00 p.m.

Directions
- *Alligator Point*; off US 98, one mile south of Ochlockonee Bay. Turn left on SR 370, travel approximately 5 miles to Bald Point Road. Turn left onto Bald Point Road and travel approximately 3 miles to the Sunrise Beach parking area.

Your dog will love the wide open spaces on the road-trails at Bald Point.

The Walks

Bring your dog for miles of wilderness hiking in these undeveloped pine flatwoods. You'll find long stretches of open-air spaces and routes through shady oak thickets. This is a free-form adventure on a maze of packed sand road-trails and narrow foot-paths.

Bald Point is lubricated by Big Chaires Creek, a prominent tidal creek bisecting the northern portion of the property that reaches into Tucker Lake, creating rich coastal marshes. This is flat, easy going for your dog throughout and even more important than most Northwest Florida parks, don't forget the insect repellent.

Trail Sense: You can print a trailmap off the Internet but you won't find one at the trailhead. Some of the routes are blazed but there is nothing to reference them against. Come to Bald Point with a spirit to explore.

Dog Friendliness

Dogs are welcome on the west side of Bald Point Road where the trails are but not on the beaches of Apalachee Bay.

Traffic

The trails are open to bikes and horses but you will find hours of solitary foot travel here.

Canine Swimming

Alligators are present in Tucker Lake and other ponds on the property. A good place to take your dog swimming is the boat ramp in the Ochlockonee Bay at the southern tip of the US 98 bridge.

Trail Time

Many hours possible.

26
Econfina River State Park

The Park

Confederate deserters during the Civil War camped along the Econfina River - with the Gulf of Mexico just beyond the salt marshes the men couldn't flee much farther south. Once here, the deserters fell in with the Union troops blockading the Florida coast, delivering fresh food and strategic information to Federal gunboats.

Settlement along the Econfina River in the 1900s was propelled by the striped mullet that would become a mainstay on local menus. Mullet does not keep well after it is caught and was salted, packed in barrels and shipped from fish camps here.

Taylor
Phone Number - (850) 922-607
Website - www.floridastateparks.org/ econfinariver
Admission Fee - None
Park Hours - Sunrise to sunset
Directions - *Lamont*; south on CR 14 across US 98 to the end.

In the 1940s, US 98 was paved and wide-ranging harvesting of timber began, with horses still employed to move trees around. In 1988 the state purchased the first of the land that would become the 4,543-acre park. Econfina River today is a linchpin in protecting one of the last stretches of unspoiled coastline in Florida.

The Walks

Econfina River State Park boasts more than nine miles of multi-use trails but most of it is a single thread that weaves through the marshes and woodlands and is better suited for long-distance riders. Canine hikers not looking a three-hour tour will favor a short stacked-loop that leaves from the boat ramp and covers a bit more than one mile. The loop can be closed with a short hike down the lightly traveled CR 14.

However long you decide to hike, you can expect to enjoy near solitude in this remote park. The path is wide and sandy but not enthusiastically maintained. This is typically not an obstacle except on the tidal marshes. It can be slow going at times but that will give you a chance to study the isolated islands dotting the grassy wetlands.

Trail Sense: The trails are blazed, a park map is available and mile posts are on the route.

Dog Friendliness
Dogs are allowed throughout the park.
Traffic
The trails are open to horses and bikes.
Canine Swimming
There is no easy access to the Econfina River.
Trail Time
Several hours available.

The low-lying trail along the salt marshes is an unmaintained jeep road where your dog can expect wet conditions.

27
Three Rivers State Park

The Park

The three rivers in question are the Flint and Chattahoochee that flow down 30 odd miles from Georgia to merge into the Apalachicola. The rivers pretty much went their own ways - including over their banks - until the 1930s when James Woodruff, a successful Georgia engineer, financier, businessman and philanthropist took a hard look at the rivers. He envisioned a waterway that would provide needed flood control, electrical power and recreation for millions of citizens living and working in this area.

Woodruff successfully agitated in Washington D.C. for the creation of the Apalachicola-Chattahoochee-Flint Project. Appropriately, the first dam built under this project was the Jim Woodruff Dam which was dedicated on March 22, 1957. Suddenly the Georgia-Florida border had a lake with 37,500 acres of water and 376 miles of shoreline. Two miles of that Lake Seminole shorleine became Three Rivers State Park.

Jackson

Phone Number
- (850) 482-9006

Website
- www.floridastateparks.org/threerivers

Admission Fee
- Vehicle parking fee

Park Hours
- 8:00 a.m. to sunset

Directions
- *Sneads*; two miles north of town of CR 271. Take Exit 158 off I-10 and go north on SR 286 to Sneads.

The Walks

This low-key park attracts mostly folks seeking recreation on the lake so when you bring your dog you can expect a quiet time on the two oft-overlooked nature trails. The *Lakeside Trail* takes off from the campground and scoots in a loop above Lake Seminole, although the woodlands are more of a feature of this half-hour hike than the water.

The *Half-Dry Creek Nature Trail* climbs across the ravines cut by those waterless streams a long time ago. Not all have played out completely so your dog can splash on a hot day during a brisk trot here. All the canine hiking in

Three Rivers meanders under mixed pines and hardwoods in classic woodland style. If your dog is enjoying this peaceful outing you can extend your visit on the yellow-blazed *Eagle Loop*.

Trail Sense: There are no maps available in the park but the trails are blazed and there are junction signs.

Your dog is likely to be frustrated finding a way into Lake Seminole, with the vegetation growing along its shore.

Dog Friendliness

Dogs are allowed on the trails, in the picnic areas and the campground.

Traffic

Foot traffic only on the nature trails.

Canine Swimming

Access to Lake Seminole is problematic - the shore is above the waterline and the edges are filled with vegetation.

Trail Time

More than one hour.

28
St. Andrews State Park

The Park

When the Spanish first settled this area they named it "St. Andres." When the British arrived they called it "Old Town" before switching over to St. Andrews in 1855.

Around this time, malaria became epidemic in America and "sea baths" were prescribed in the shallow St. Andrews Bay to restore health. When the War Between The States erupted, St. Andrews was a strategic supplier of salt to the Confederate troops. More than 2,000 men were engaged in producing the critical preservative, which sold for as much as fifty dollars per bushel. Federal raids were directed against the salt works beginning in September of 1862 but the Floridians rebuilt as soon as Union forces departed and the works remained operational through the end of the Civil War.

War again visited St. Andrews during World War II when the area was part of St. Andrews Military Reservation. After the war ended, the park opened in 1951 and now consists of more than 1,260 acres.

Bay
Phone Number - (850) 233-5140
Website - www.floridastateparks.org/standrews
Admission Fee - Vehicle entrance fee
Park Hours - 8:00 a.m. to sunset
Directions - *Panama City*; from US 98 turn south on Thomas Drive (SR 3031) and follow it to SR 392. Turn left to enter into the park.

The Walks

While most visitors to St. Andrews State Park head straight for the sugary white sands that have been called "the most beautiful beach in the world" you and your dog will make a left turn and set off for the mostly ignored Grand Lagoon side of the park. Starting at a re-created turpentine still, set off on a rollicking exploration of the scrubby dunes on the *Heron Pond Trail*. High in the dunes your dog can at least look down and see some of that celebrated Gulf of Mexico shoreline. The route touches against the Grand Lagoon where canine hikers can enjoy a narrow strip of sand and leisurely swimming in the shallow, gentle waters.

Closer to the crowds is the *Gator Lake Trail*, a surprisingly quiet half-mile trail through a sandy waste area on the edge of the park. Most of the hiking in the park is exposed to the sun so keep your dog's water handy when it's hot.

Trail Sense: A park map is available but don't panic if you don't have one.

Dog Friendliness

Dogs are allowed on the trails but not on the swimming beaches.

Traffic

Foot traffic only on the nature trails; you can hike the open park roads as well but look for vehicles and bikes.

Canine Swimming

The Grand Lagoon can be deep enough for dog paddling.

Trail Time

About one hour.

29
Eden Gardens
State Park

The Park

This property on the south shore of Tucker Bayou was home to the Wesley Lumber Company during Florida's first timber boom prior to World War I. In addition to a sawmill, planer mill and dry kiln, there was a cluster of about 20 company-owned homes where the workers lived. A dock extended into Tucker Bayou where barges were loaded with freshly milled pine and cypressboards.

William Henry Wesley built a mansion home at his mill in 1895, said to be modeled after an antebellum plantation house where he was given shelter on his return from the War Between the States. The 5,500-foot house started a design trend that influenced the entire Florida Panhandle at the time. Its two stories, divided by a central hallway on both floors, was ideal for allowing cooling breezes to blow through the house before the advent of air conditioning. Being built on piers also made the house safe when Tucker Bayou or Choctawhatchee Bay periodically flooded the area.

Walton
Phone Number - (850) 231-4214
Website - www.floridastateparks.org/ edengardens
Admission Fee - Vehicle entrance fee
Park Hours - 8:00 a.m. to sunset
Directions - *Point Washington*; between Destin and Panama City Beach take CR 395 north from US 98. The park is one mile on the left.

The Walks

Most visitors to Eden Gardens come to tour the sparkling white mansion, donated by the last owner, Lois Maxon, to the state in 1968. In fact, it would appear there would not be much for a dog owner here. Perhaps a short stroll on the *Garden Trail* under moss-draped oaks with a stop at the small beach by the old mill site on Tucker Bayou.

It is a welcome surprise, therefore, to stumble on a nature trail through the forest in the western section of the property that isn't even listed on the park map. This delightful serpentine path winds through mature woods, serving up roomy and easy trotting for your dog. A highlight is a small, sandy beach on the Tucker Bayou where your dog can cool off.

A stroll around Eden Gardens' ornamental grounds is a highlight for any dog.

Trail Sense: No trail map, but once on the trail small signs point the way.

Dog Friendliness
Dogs are welcome on the grounds but not in the Wesley House.

Traffic
Foot traffic only and 8 times out of 10 you will be alone on the nature trail.

Canine Swimming
There is enough clear water in the bayou for your dog to safely step in.

Trail Time
About one hour.

30
Blackwater River State Park

The Park

The Blackwater River flows down 45 miles from its source in Alabama picking up tannins from tree bark and decaying plant material as it goes. The organic matter stains the water a tea color but the water itself is some of the purest of any sandbottom river in the world. The white sandbar beaches, dark water and vibrant greenery form an unforgettable kaleidoscope in the park, which was opened in 1968 with 360 acres.

The Walks

The star of the park is the Blackwater River that moseys along at about two miles per hour with an average depth of less than three feet. As a result there is often more traffic out on the water - the river is a designated *Florida Canoe Trail* - than on the trails. And this is an ideal place to bring your dog paddling.

For canine hikers, there are two trails of choice, the more tempting being the *Chain of Lakes Nature Trail*. This path begins by mimicking the twists of the Blackwater River before exploring the upland pine forests. Be aware that this pathway is subject to high water and becomes impassable when wet.

At the campground your dog can jump on the shortish *Juniper Lake Trail* that visits a small oxbow lake, water that was once a part of the river that became stranded when the main channel cut a straighter course. Ambitious trail dogs can also use the park as a jumping off point for the *Juniper Creek Trail*, a section of the *Florida Trail* that runs eight miles to Red Rock Road. The most interesting

Santa Rosa

Phone Number
- (850) 983-5363

Website
- www.floridastateparks.org/blackwaterriver

Admission Fee
- Yes, a parking fee

Park Hours
- 8:00 a.m. to sunset

Directions
- *Harold*; west of Holt. Travel on US 90 to Deaton Bridge Road, turn right and continue 3 miles to the park. A lot for the *Chain of Lakes Nature Trail* is on the left before crossing the Blackwater River.

part of this hike comes two miles from the park when you cross Indian Ford
Road and begin a long waterside journey beside the Juniper Creek.

Trail Sense: The *Juniper Creek Trail* is well-blazed; the shorter park trails
are navigated via trailmap.

Dog Friendliness

Dogs are allowed to hike the trail and stay the night in the campground
but can not go on the beaches.

Traffic

Foot traffic only and generally not heavy outside the campground loop.

Canine Swimming

There are places for your dog to slip into the Blackwater River from the trail
away from the sand beaches.

Trail Time

Less than an hour to a full day possible.

31
Big Lagoon State Park

The Park

This 712-acre park opened on the north shore of Big Lagoon, which separates the mainland from Perdido Key, in 1978 and rapidly became a favorite destination for campers, boaters and fishermen.

In Septemeber of 2004 when Hurrican Ivan made landfall its highest windspeeds of 130 mph occurred right here. The storm surge left the park office under four feet of water. Park staff and hundreds of volunteers worked tirelessly to bring the park back to life, with many facilities made available in just a few weeks.

Escambia

Phone Number
- (850) 492-1595

Website
- www.floridastateparks.org/biglagoon

Admission Fee
- Vehicle entrance fee

Park Hours
- 8:00 a.m. to sunset

Directions
- *Pensacola*; 10 miles southwest of town. From US 98 take CR 293 south to its end at Gulf Beach Highway, CR 292A, and the park entrance across the road.

The Walks

The original star walk in the park, the *Cookie Trail*, was developed and maintained by local Girl Scouts. It was a watery exploration through scrub oak forest that visited the main park features: the Grand Lagoon, the Big Lagoon and Long Pond. Since Hurricane Ivan the route has been salvaged in enough places to create the *Sand Pine Trail*, that moves through the salt marshes and sandy expanse around the lagoon, and the *Estuary Trail* that makes extensive use of boardwalks.

Away from the coast, on the north side of the park road, a narrow, 1.5-mile trail scoots through a shady pine forest sprinkled with live oaks and saw palmettos. All the canine hiking at Big Lagoon is easy going and ideal for a languid day out with your dog.

Trail Sense: Old trails mingle with new routes but any confusion is soon mitigated by the compactness of the hiking area.

The state park affords several vantage points for your dog to observe Big Lagoon, including traffic using the Intracoastal Waterway.

Dog Friendliness
Dogs are permitted on the trails and in the campgrounds but cannot go on any swimming beach.

Traffic
Even on busy days you can find solitude on these footpaths.

Canine Swimming
There are places to slip into the water at Big Lagoon State Park but alligators do make their home here.

Trail Time
More than one hour.

32
St. Joseph Peninsula State Park

The Park

Things have always had trouble taking hold on this lengthy sand spit extending out from Cape San Blas. When the Spanish were squabbling with the French and British in the early 1700s they built a fort, Presidio San Jose, at the tip of the peninsula but the settlers soon abandoned the fort.

The British took control in the 1800s and built a lighthouse on St. Joseph's Point in 1839 to promote shipping in the bay. But after the town's population was decimated by yellow fever in 1841, the lighthouse was dismantled.

Appropriately the Stone family was able to purchase the peninsula for delinquent taxes in 1868. So when Terrell Higdon (T.H.) Stone arrived in 1904 at the age of 36 to claim his substantial acreage around St. Joseph Bay his was the first house built in what would become Port St. Joe. T. H. Stone looked around, saw nothing but timber and went into the turpentine business. He hauled barrels of distilled resin to Pensacola on the *Miss Steppie*, which can still be seen in the town harbor today. When St. Joseph Peninsula State Park opened in 1967, it was named in honor of the founding father and long-time mayor of Port St. Joe.

Gulf
Phone Number - (850) 227-1327
Website - www.floridastateparks.org/ stjoseph
Admission Fee - Vehicle entrance fee
Park Hours - 8:00 a.m. to sunset
Directions - *Port St. Joe*; From US 98 take SR 30A to Cape San Blas Road and travel 10 miles to the park entrance.

The Walks

Although remote, St. Joseph Peninsula can be a busy place with camping, boating, fishing, picnicking and even a playground. Things are not so hectic on the park's nature trails that visit the heavily forested interior between the bay and the gulf and break into the open along St. Joseph Bay.

Most of your dog's hiking here will be on impossibly white sands that can get thick enough to produce a good workout. Your explorations will have to end at the beginning of the St. Joseph Wilderness Preserve however - no dogs allowed there.

Trail Sense: Not much help beyond the trailhead but it won't matter.

There is plenty of room for your dog to stretch out on the white sand trails along St. Joseph Bay.

Dog Friendliness
Dogs are not permitted on the beach, in the campground or in the St. Joseph Wilderness Preserve that stretches for 7.5 miles beyond the developed area of the park.

Traffic
Foot traffic only on the nature trails.

Canine Swimming
Try the boat ramp along St. Joseph Bay if it is not busy.

Trail Time
More than one hour.

33

Gulf Islands National Seashore –
Fort Pickens

The Park

Fort Pickens occupies the western tip of Santa Rosa Island and was the largest of a series of forts built to protect Pensacola harbor. Constructed with 21.5 million bricks, the pentagonal bastion was completed in 1834. It would be occupied off and on until 1947.

Fort Pickens saw much early action in the Civil War after the lightly fortified Federal naval yard in Pensacola was given over to the Rebels. Fort Pickens was able to be supplied by sea so the Union company held out. After testing artillery battles, two warships drove the Confederates from two sister forts on the barrier islands, Fort Barrancas and Fort McRae. On May 9, 1862, the Confederates abandoned Pensacola, and Fort Pickens, once a linchpin in the Union blockade, became a prison.

Congress established the Gulf Islands National Seashore in 1971 with Fort Pickens included as one of 11 separate units stretching from West Ship Island, Mississippi to Santa Rosa Island.

Santa Rosa
Phone Number - (850) 934-2600
Website - www.nps.gov/guis
Admission Fee - Vehicle entrance fee
Park Hours - 8:00 a.m. to sunset
Directions - *Pensacola Beach*; take SR 399 south from US 98 onto Santa Rosa Island and turn right on Fort Pickens Road to the park.

The Walks

In 2004, Hurricane Ivan, which at the time set a record for 36 consecutive six hour periods at Category 4 strength, swamped Santa Rosa Island. Fort Pickens Road into the park has been closed ever since with a scheduled re-opening of 2009. In the meantime, dog owners can hike down the road and enjoy the solitude of the barrier island.

For many, the name Geronimo is synonomous with the American West and the subjugation of the native tribes. But the legendary Apache leader's story is not complete without his chapter at Fort Pickens. Geronimo was a Bedonkohe Apache who married into the Arizona Chiricahuas. After his mother, wife and children were murdered by Mexican soldiers in 1858, the 29-year old medicine man (he was never a chief) vowed revenge and led a marauding band of Apaches against settlers and the Army for the next three decades. Geronimo was eventually betrayed by Apache scouts and captured at Skeleton Canyon in 1886. The entire Chiricahua tribe was herded onto trains and shipped into exile to Florida. The Apaches were to be sent to St. Augustine but several Pensacola civic leaders, with dollar signs in their heads, convinced the government to hold Geronimo at Fork Pickens, that had been vacant and decaying since the Civil War. The proud and famous Indian leader was thus reduced to tourist sideshow. As many as 459 gawkers visited on one day and the typical daily crowd was at least 20. Pensacola reaped the benefits of his imprisonment for 18 months. Geronimo continued his strange odyssey as a prisoner/curiousity, appearing at the 1904 St. Louis World's Fair and in President Theodore Roosevelt's Inaugural Parade. The sad final third of his life ended with his death in 1909.

In good times, the park featured two short nature trails that may be restored but this main artery - and the adjoining *Hike-Bike Trail* has always been the route of choice to see the fort and batteries and experience the sand scrub environment.

Trail Sense: None needed.

Dog Friendliness
Dogs are welcome to use the closed Fort Pickens Road but are not allowed on the beach.

Traffic
Foot traffic only until the park reopens.

Canine Swimming
None.

Trail Time
It is a four-hour roundtrip from the park entrance to the Fort Pickens.

34
Lake Jackson Mounds Archaeological State Park

The Park

The original settlers of this land between the Aucilla and Ochlockonee rivers were the Apalachee Indians. Beginning around A.D. 1000 ancestors of the Apalachees started developing ceremonial mound centers, including the one at Lake Jackson. Atop these earthen mound were built temples or homes for tribal leaders.

At its peak, the Lake Jackson Mound complex consisted of six temple mounds and a large village circling a central plaza. Scattered farmsteads surrounded the area. The area was abandoned sometime around A.D. 1500 as the community migrated elsewhere.

In Florida's nascent period before 1860, the land was part of a bustling cotton plantation owned by Colonel Robert Butler, who received the surrender of East Florida from the Spaniards on July 10, 1821 and was appointed Florida's first Surveyor General by Governor Andrew Jackson.

Today the Lake Jackson Mounds have proved to be one the richest troves of prehistoric artifacts and burial objects in Florida.

Leon

Phone Number
- (850) 922-6007

Website
- www.floridastateparks.org/lakejacksonmounds

Admission Fee
- Vehicle parking fee

Park Hours
- 8:00 a.m. to sunset

Directions
- *Tallahassee*; from Exit 199 off I-10, head north on US 27. After two miles turn right on Crowder Road and continue to park entrance on right.

The Walks

For a tranquil outing with your dog, Lake Jackson Mounds has few peers. An interpretive trail leads through a large, open grassy area containing the remnants of the ceremonial mounds. Ideal for a game of fetch or even a picnic with your dog.

A nature trail prowls around a wooded ravine and passes the remains of an 1800s grist mill. The path is roomy and soft under paw with enough elevation change to hold your dog's interest. Along the trail you'll pass several towering longleaf pines above and wildflowers beneath.

Trail Sense: There is a mapboard posted at the information kiosk and you can scout the park visually from there.

Dog Friendliness
Dogs are permitted on the trails and in the mounds area.
Traffic
What little traffic you'll encounter will be foot traffic only.
Canine Swimming
An old borrow pit is often filled with enough water for a quick doggie dip.
Trail Time
About one hour.

The largest of the ceremonial mounds at Lake Jackson is almost three stories high.

35
Blackwater Heritage State Trail

The Park

Established in 1825 as a trading post on the Blackwater River, Milton is one of the oldest towns in Florida. The lumber industry developed rapidly and by the late 1850s surrounding Santa Rosa County was the most industrialized county in the entire state.

The Bagdad Land and Lumber Company operated the short-line Florida & Alabama Railroad to haul pine logs and the occasional passenger to Whitney, Alabama. Service was discontinued when the Bagdad mill shuttered in 1939 but briefly revived to supply the newly built Whiting Field Naval Air Station during World War II. Afterwards the 44-mile route was left to the weeds forever.

The U.S. Department of Interior donated this land to the State of Florida in 1993 which developed the *Blackwater Heritage State Trail* on seven miles of the original railbed.

Santa Rosa

Phone Number
- (850) 983-5338

Website
- www.dep.state.fl.us/gwt/state/black

Admission Fee
- None

Park Hours
- 8:00 a.m. to sunset

Directions
- *Milton*; the trailhead is in town on the northeast corner of the intersection of SR 87 and US 90, just west of the junction with SR 191.

The Walks

This popular paved trail is conveniently segmented to allow canine hikes without a car shuttle. Dog owners may want to skip the first mile of the trail that runs through old Milton neighborhoods and crosses several streets. After the Visitors Center, located at Alabama and Chaffin streets, the route becomes rural and sunny, with the woods often set back from the right-of-way.

About halfway, there is a parking lot for equestrians who can use a natural trail next to the asphalt strip. There is an ample shoulder for canine hikers to use when the trail is busy with cyclists and this equestrian trail affords an excellent alternative to pounding the pavement.

At the terminus of the railbed at CR 87A the *Blackwater Heritage Trail* continues for another 1.5 miles on the *Military Heritage Trail* at Whiting Field. This is easy trotting for your dog throughout with attractive wooden fences and bridges spanning serpentine creeks.

Trail Sense: There are information kiosks and mile markers on the trail so you can gauge where you want to turn around.

Dog Friendliness
Dogs are permitted to hike the *Blackwater Heritage Trail*.

Traffic
You will see plenty of cyclists and joggers and rollerbladers and an occasional equestrian.

Canine Swimming
Despite its name, the route never touches the Blackwater River; Clear Creek and other streams are not deep enough for aquatic shenanigans beyond splashing.

Trail Time
More than one hour.

36
Fred Gannon Rocky Bayou State Park

The Park

In 1940 the United States Forestry Service gave the War Department 800 square miles of Gulf Coast dunesland and pine forests in Florida for gunnery and bombing practice. During World War II Lieutenant Colonel James Doolittle trained his B-52 squadron for its bombing missions over Japan. A concrete bomb still on park grounds is believed to have been dropped from Doolittle's planes.

After the war ended, people began moving to the Florida Gulf Coast, making it unusable as a bombing range. In the late 1950s Air Force Colonel Fred

Okaloosa

Phone Number
- (850) 833-9144

Website
- www.floridastateparks.org/rockybayou

Admission Fee
- Vehicle entrance fee

Park Hours
- 8:00 a.m. to sunset

Directions
- *Niceville*; at 4821 on SR 20, five miles east of SR 285.

Gannon, Director of Civil Engineering at Eglin Air Force Base, proposed to transform Rocky Bayou, an arm of Choctawhatchee Bay from missile target to tranquil park. Gannon designed the recreational facility and began construction with his Air Corps engineers. When the roads and trails were completed in 1966, the park was turned over to the Florida state park system.

The Walks

Known primarily as a camping and boating park, Rocky Bayou should not be overlooked by dog owners seeking a day hike. This is all easy going for your dog on three nature trails totalling four miles. The paths are flat and soft and sandy under paw.

Each of the three trails is dominated by a different ecosystem. The *Red Cedar Nature Trail* meanders across a hardwood hammock of oak, magnolia and red cedar. The *Rocky Bayou Trail* takes your dog to the edge of the bay and is spotted with old growth longleaf pines, some on the long side of 300 years old. The *Sand Pine Trail* traces Puddin Head Lake, a narrow, shallow body of water that was created by pioneer dams and reformed by active beavers.

Trail Sense: Wayfinding is not a problem on these loops; a park map and interpretive brochure is available.

Dog Friendliness
Dogs are allowed to enjoy these trails and stay in the campground.
Traffic
Most visitors to Rocky Bayou are eager to get out on the water, land-lovers will be in a distinct minority.
Canine Swimming
The bayou and Puddin Head Lake are not suitable for canine aquatics with alligators lurking in the shallow water.
Trail Time
More than one hour.

37
Ponce de Leon Springs State Park

The Park

In 1513, Juan Ponce de Leon, one year from being deposed as governor of Puerto Rico, equipped three ships at his own expense and set off on a voyage of conquest and discovery. He soon landed on the northeast coast of present-day Florida, which he claimed for Spain and named "flowery."

He would return in 1521. Legend has it Ponce was seeking a mythical "fountain of youth" but he was accompanied by 200 farmers and artisans and a host of barnyard animals on a colonizing voyage. Instead of discovering immortality, Ponce took home a wound from an Indian arrow from which he would die. He never visited the spring that was named for him almost 500 years later.

Holmes

Phone Number
- (850) 836-4281

Website
- www.floridastateparks.org/poncedeleonsprings

Admission Fee
- Vehicle entrance fee

Park Hours
- 8:00 a.m to sunset

Directions
- *Ponce de Leon*; take Exit 96 off I-10 and go north to US 90. Turn right and again at the next right on CR 181A to park.

The spring is a confluence of two underground flows that send 14 million gallons of water to the surface every day. Local residents have gathered at the spot for recreation for generations and it did not become an official park until the property was acquired by the state in 1970.

The Walks

Water, as one might expect, is the dominant feature of your dog's day at Ponce de Leon Springs State Park. The spring connects with Sandy Creek, Mill Creek and Blue Creek as they flow into the Choctawhatchee River and on into the Gulf of Mexico. Two short nature trails tour the floodplain between all these streams.

The *Spring Run Trail* is a double loop that hugs the quick-moving Sandy Creek under a scruffy canopy of holly, oak and moss-draped cypress. Under paw

Your dog can look - but now swim - in Ponce de Leon Springs.

the going can get muddy and is rooty enough to keep your dog high-stepping along the way.

The highlight of the *Sandy Creek Loop* comes when the clear spring water meets the turbid waters of Sandy Creek. A longer hike than its cousin across the spring, a cypress swamp is tossed into the aquatic mix here. Aside from the roots, this is easy hiking for any dog on both trails.

Trail Sense: There is nothing beyond trailhead signs to guide you but that is all you really need.

Dog Friendliness
Dogs are not permitted in the swimming area.
Traffic
Foot traffic only in this laid-back park; don't expect to be elbowing folks off the trail to get by.
Canine Swimming
Alligators are present in Sandy Creek but there are places of clear water in the streams where your dog can cool off.
Trail Time
About one hour.

38
Henderson Beach State Park

The Park

In the early 1830s, Leonard Destin, his father George, and brother William set out from New London, Connecticut with three ships to fish along the East Coast. The expedition ran into a hurricane near Cape Canaveral, Florida and lost two ships, carrying George and William to the bottom of the sea.

With little left to return to, Leonard continued on and settled here in 1835 to fish. Despite his quarter-century of residency, he was nearly hung as a spy during the War Between the States, spared only by a judge who was a fellow mason.

By his death in 1884, Destin had built a thriving commercial fishery. One of the deckhands he hired was a diligent 13 year-old named William Marler. Over the years Captain "Uncle Billy" Marler became a prime mover in the nascent fishing village and named it after the founder, Leonard Destin.

As the closest spot on the Gulf to deep water, modern-day Destin has earned the monicker of "The Luckiest Fishing Village in the World." With development threatening to swallow the the shore, two local high-schoolers, Jeff Crumpler and Cliff Reynolds, revived interested in creating a park. Governor Bob Graham endorsed the idea and in 1983, Destin landowner Burney Henderson, whose family had owned the property since the 1930s, sold 208 acres of his property to Florida for $13.1 million. It was the state's first land purchase under the Save Our Coasts program.

Holmes
Phone Number - (850) 837-7550
Website - www.floridastateparks.org/ hendersonbeach
Admission Fee - Vehicle entrance fee
Park Hours - 8:00 a.m to sunset
Directions - *Destin*; located in the city on US 98, 1.5 miles west of Toll Road 293 (Mid-Bay Bridge).

The Walks

There is only one trail at Henderson Beach but it is a beauty - a .75-mile rollercoaster hike through the coastal beach dunes. You start high enough to see the emerald green Gulf waters that your dog can't get to and drop into the sheltered dunes that are evergreen and fragrant with rosemary and sand pines. In these dunes is as close to shade as your dog will find in the entire park. The surface is all sand with wood chips mixed in, so nice your dog will want to go around twice.

Trail Sense: The trail leaves from behind the playground and finishes in the same spot without consternation.

Dog Friendliness
The *Nature Trail* is dog-friendly and so are the campgrounds but dogs can not go on the boardwalk or the beach.

Traffic
This is a busy park in-season and some traffic may actually spill from the beach onto the trail; foot travel only.

Canine Swimming
Nope.

Trail Time
Less than one hour.

Hiking with your dog on the Henderson Beach **Nature Trail** *is like wandering though nature's art gallery.*

39
St. Joseph Bay
State Buffer Preserve

The Park

In 1969 the St. Joseph Bay Aquatic Preserve was established to protect the important natural resources of St. Joseph Bay. Recognizing the importance of surrounding uplands to the preservation of the outstanding water quality and natural resources of the bay, the St. Joseph Bay State Buffer Preserve was created in 1995 with an initial 702 acres that has grown to more than 5,000 acres on three tracts.

The Walks

The main Buffer tract, across the road from the Preserves Center, are a spiderweb of sandy woods roads that make up the Preserve trail system. There are no improved trails and things can get wild and wooly, especially when it is wet. But, if you are looking for a solitary place to hike with your dog, you will find it here.

Treasure Road is the primary road that runs across the spine of the property for three miles. This hard-packed, graded sandy path will promise the most reliable footing and is an enjoyable trot for your dog on a wide, level path. The landscape is flat pinelands that are burned regularly to keep the natural communities of plants and animals healthy. The abundance of rare plants make the St. Joseph Buffer Preserve a particularly attractive spring destination.

Trail Sense: A trailmap is available, either at the trailhead or outside the Preserve office. Nothing is marked so leave Treasure Road only with an a spirit of adventure.

Gulf
Phone Number - (850) 229-1787
Website - www.dep.state.fl.us/coastal/ sites/apalachicola/stjoseph_ buffer.htm
Admission Fee - None
Park Hours - 8:00 a.m. to sunset
Directions - *Port St. Joe*; on CR 30, five miles south of US 98 to the parking area on the east side of the road.

Dog Friendliness
Dogs are permitted to hike in the Preserve.

Traffic
Bikes and horses are allowed on the main roads only; if you share these trails with anyone it will probably be birdwatchers.

Canine Swimming
Alligators are present in the park waters.

Trail Time
More than one hour.

40
Tallahassee–St. Marks Historic Railroad State Trail

The Park

In 1824 Tallahassee was chosen as the site for the Florida Territorial capital. Eleven years later wooden tracks were laid to the coastal town of St. Marks and in 1837 the state's first railroad, pulled by mules, was in operation. In 1856 the wooden rails were pulled up and replaced with steel and soon locomotives were busy transporting Confederate troops between the Gulf of Mexico and Tallahassee during the Civil War. But for most of its history the line hauled cotton, timber and naval stores.

The Tallahassee-St. Marks Railroad would trundle on for most of the 20th century until 1983, gaining recognition as Florida's longest operating rail line. This would certainly have stunned one early traveler who, after enduring a trip on the rickety wooden railbed proclaimed the Tallahassee-St. Marks Railroad as, "the worst that has yet been built in the entire world."

In 1986 the State of Florida allocated funds to convert the Sunshine State's first railroad into its first rail-trail. In 1988 the *Tallahassee-St. Marks Historic Railroad State Trail* was dedicated at opening ceremonies in Woodville.

Wakulla/Leon
Phone Number - (850) 245-2052
Website - www.floridastateparks.org/ standrews
Admission Fee - None
Park Hours - Sunrise to sunset
Directions - *Tallahassee*; from downtown, take Monroe Street south. It will turn into Woodville Highway (SR 363). After you pass Capital Circle (US 319), look for trailhead on right.

The Walks

Canine hikers will want to tackle the southern legs of this 16-mile route to avoid the hustle and bustle of the capital where the venerable right-o-way clings to busy Route 363 for quite a distance. Closer to St. Marks the trail has a more rural feel, often pinched by trees as it passes Apalachicola State Forest.

For much of its distance the 8-foot wide strip of pavement is flanked by a dirt horse trail which will usually be the surface of choice for your dog. The *Tallahassee-St. Marks Trail* is uniformly flat and remarkably straight almost the entire way. Bring plenty of drinking water if you plan an extended outing on the historic railroad.

At several junctions you can detour off the strip onto dirt trails that lead into the woods for a change of pace. These trails, such as *Munson Hills*, were designed for off-road biking so stay alert.

Trail Sense: There are distance aids and maps posted at the various stops alogn the rail trail.

Dog Friendliness
Dogs are allowed to hike the *Tallahassee-St. Marks Trail*.

Traffic
You may chance to see any type of non-motorized locomotion with wheels here: bikes, strollers, skates. There are plenty of trail users - especially on a nice weekend day.

Canine Swimming
None.

Trail Time
Many hours possible.

41
University of West Florida

Escambia County

From I-10 take Exit 13 North on SR 291, North Davis Highway; after crossing SR 290 turn left on University Parkway and continue to the Welcome Center across US 90 at 11000 University Parkway, Building 81

The University of West Florida in Pensacola was chartered by the Florida Legislature in 1955 with the first students attending classes in 1967. The entire 1,600-acre campus, the second largest in the state system, has been designated a nature preserve. A canine hike across campus is divided into three areas and is reserved for foot traffic only - no off-road vehicles or mountain bikes permitted.

The highlight of the tour is a half-mile boardwalk in the Edward Ball Nature Preserve that visits a hardwood swamp on a wooden boardwalk. The trail through the central campus is a mix of the natural and the manicured, passing by impressive specimens of magnolia, dogwood, azalea and oak. The final stations are in the sandhills, hardwood hammocks and wetlands of the Baars-Firestone Wildlife Sanctuary, set off from the main campus a bit. You can easily spend over an hour with your dog in this garden-like setting.

42
Garcon Point Trails

Santa Rosa County

On CR 191 off CR 281, south of I-10, Exit 22

Surrounded by bays on three sides, this land was purchased by Northwest Florida Water Management District to protect water quality. There are two tail-friendly sand trails here: a 1.5-mile loop with a mile-long spur.

Expect to get your shoes wet and to wade in some places. The paths wander through low-lying wet prairie and flatwoods and the water can overwhelm the trail in spots. This is and ideal environment for orchids and hungry insectivorous plants such as sundews, butterworts, pitcher plants and bladderworts. The scruffy woodlands and open grass passages give your dog plenty of chance to sniff the salty breezes.

43
Aucilla Wildlife Management Area
Jefferson County and Taylor County

From the intersection of CR 14 and US 98 drive west two miles to Powell Hammock Road and turn right; go 4.4 miles to Goose Pasture Road (FR #5049) and turn left - parking will be one mile on the right

For over 12,000 years Indians made use of the Wacissa and Aucilla rivers to hunt and fish. Big game could be found here - in 1993, archeologists from the University of Florida recovered a 7.5-foot mastodon tusk from a site along the Aucilla River. Eight long cut marks at the point where the tusk emerged from the skull indicated that it had been removed from the skull by humans. Radiocarbon dated the tusk at 12,200 years ago, one of the earliest records of human activity in North America.

Recreation within the 47,532-acre Aucilla Wildlife Management Area, where land acquisitions began in 1988, comes complements of the two sparkling rivers. Canoes and kayaks are a staple on the pristine Wacissa River, where you can swim or snorkel in one of the many springs that feed the river. The Aucilla is more often used for hiking.

On either side of Goose Pasture Road a seven-mile chunk of the *Florida National Scenic Trail* traces the Aucilla Sinks. About a half-mile north of the road the swamp-fed river disappears into a limestone tunnel. For the rest of this canine hike your dog will be wondering what happened to the stream he was following as the Aucilla River reappears and goes away again. There are dozens of limestone sinkholes to explore along this route. Enough dolomitic limestone remains that it is still actively mined here.

44
Tom Brown Park

Leon County
In downtown Tallahassee on Easterwood Road, off US 319

Originally a prison farm, the land for the 255-acre park was acquired by Leon County in 1971. Tallahassee's largest recreational park on the south shore of Upper Lake Lafayette has plenty to offer a visiting dog. The paved *Goose Pond Trail* traces the lakeshore across the entirety of the park for 1.5 miles and leads right to the city dog park.

Inside the two fenced areas, one for large dogs and one for smaller scamps, are benches, poopbags, water - and trees. Right next door, by Leon Lake you can play disc golf with your dog in tow.

If hiking on concrete is your thing, the park also connects to the *Cadillac Trail* down shore to Lafayette Heritage Trail Park. The park also maintains natural trails for mountain biking on the *Magnolia Trails*. If you venture into this area of the park your dog will find enough hills that European Olympic teams used these trails to train for the 1996 Atlanta Olympics. Start with the easy-going *K-9 Loop*.

45
Joe Budd Wildlife Management Area
Gadsden County

From I-10, Exit 192, take US 90 2.1 miles to SR 268, make a left and continue to the entrance on Peters Road on the left

In 1975, the State of Florida purchased 794 acres from tobacco baron Joseph T. Budd Jr., manufacturer of "Florida Queen" cigars. Budd raised Tennessee Walking Horses, including Old Glory's Man, a classy sorrel stallion who became the winner of the Grand Championship Stake from outside the State of Tennessee in 1950.

An additional 4000 acres were later leased from Florida Power Corporation, and today the Florida Fish and Wildlife Conservation Commission manages 11,039 acres on the north shore of Lake Talquin. The Joe Budd Management Area is renowned for its weekend hunts that attract sportsmen from around the state.

But that leaves more than 300 days a year when the area is closed to hunting and the extensive network of lightly-used packed sand roads are open to canine hiking, biking and equestrians. At the Joe Budd Aquatic Education Center the *Wetland Nature Trail* explores a cypress swamp.

46
Deer Lake State Park
Santa Rosa County

On CR 30A in Sant Rosa Beach.

Deer Lake State Park is a 1,920-acre facility on the Gulf of Mexico named after a freshwater coastal dune lake within its boundaries. Dogs are not allowed on the beach but can go to the picnic area and on the nature trail across Route 30A. There is no place to park at the trailhead so you will need to walk back up the park entrance road (currently no fee in this small lot).

Tucked into major seaside developments, this diminutive park is seldom crowded. You can poke around the dunes a bit with your dog before reaching the prohibited beach or head into the thick woodlands on the north side of the road. The limited trails of Deer Lake connect with those in Point Washington State Forest for extended hiking time with your dog.

47
Box-R Wildlife Management Area
Franklin County
Off US 98, six miles west of Apalachicola with entrances off CR 385 and CR 384

The wilderness between the new communities of Port St. Joe and Apalachicola was breached in 1909 when the Apalachicola and Northern Railroad built sixteen miles of track across what is now the Box-R Wildlife Management Area. The Box-R was originally the private ranch of Edward Ball, co-founder of the St. Joe Company. Visitors hunted the woods for deer, hog and turkey.

There are no formal trails across the 8,397 protected acres but when the area is closed to hunting (all but about 50 days a year) you can hike with your dog along 20 miles of existing roads. Fall is the most popular time to hike Box-R when the colorful foliage of the deciduous gums, red maples and cypress trees paints the landscape. Deep into the road/trails you will bring your dog to several openings along more than a mile of frontage on the Jackson and Apalachicola rivers.

48
Econfina Creek Water Management Area
Washington County and Bay County
West Entrance of Florida National Scenic Trail *is on SR 20, west of US 231; the East Entrance is west of US 231 on Scott Road via Sweetwater Creek Road*

The lure for canine hikers to this 41,000-acre area that drains the Econfina Creek basin is a 14-mile segment of the *Florida National Scenic Trail*. The footpath traverses remnant old growth native longleaf pine and wiregrass communities in a region that was heavily logged and and planted with commercial stands of non-native sand and slash pine. Along the creek hardwood forests and hammocks also grow above fern-covered limestone bluffs and outcrops. In the spring, blooming dogwoods, snow white mountain laurel and wild azaleas decorate the trail.

This is a full backpacking excursion through natural, rolling sandhills for your dog - there are no take-outs along the trail and without a car shuttle the only day-hiking will be out-and-back. At Pitt Spring (on SR 20, east of the trailhead) your dog can sample the watershed's pure lakes on a shortish nature trail, ideal for a doggie dip.

49
Dead Lakes State Recreation Area
Gulf County
One mile north of Wewahitchka on SR 71

The Dead Lakes supposedly formed ages ago when sand bars created by the current of the Apalachicola River blocked the Chipola River. The ensuing high water killed thousands of trees in the floodplain, giving the area its name.

From 1936 until 1951, the Game Commission operated the area as a fish hatchery. Two ponds and one of the two houses built for the resident biologist in 1936 still remain in the park. In the 1950s much of the upland pinetums were tapped for turpentine; a still was located just beyond the current park boundary.

The Department of Natural Resources subleased this 83-acre area from the Florida Game and Fresh Water Fish Commission in 1974. There are two nature hikes in the park; one around the open banks of the man-made ponds to the edge of the Dead Lakes and the other through the woodlands adjacent to the campground. "Hands-off" appears to be the maintenance philosophy here - expect to fight your way through blowdowns on the trail.

This is not a "Dead Lake" but a man-made one in the park.

101

50
Taking Your Dog
To The Roof Of Florida

Highpointers are folks who seek to stand atop the highest point in each of the 50 states. The first person known to have tagged the summits of the 48 contiguous states was a fellow named Arthur Marshall back in 1936. After Hawaii and Alaska were added to the union in the 1950s, Vin Hoeman became the person to reach the top of all 50 states. To date fewer than 200 people have been documented to have climbed - as the case may be - all 50 highpoints.

Your dog can be a Highpointer too. She can't complete all the peaks - there are places she can't go legally (the spectacular Mount Katahdin at the northern terminus of the Appalachian Trail in Maine, for instance), mountains she can't climb physically (the vertical rock climbs at the top of Gannett Peak in Montana), or both (Mount McKinley, the highest of American peaks at over 20,000 feet). But that leaves plenty of state summits for your dog to experience.

The highest mountain in America's Lower 48 is California's Mount Whitney at 14,494 feet. But the hike to the top is not arduous and so popular permits are rationed out to get on the trail. You can hike with your dog to the shadow of the summit but the final steps will be yours alone as you leave the dog-friendly Inyo National Forest and travel into Sequoia National Park, where dogs are banned from the trails.

That leaves as the highest spot in America where your dog is allowed to go Mount Elbert in Colorado, only 61 feet lower than Whitney. Luckily, the hike to the top is again a relatively easy one and plenty of dogs make the day-trip every year. The round trip is between 9 and 15 miles, depending on how close to the trailhead your vehicle can get you, and there is no rock scrambling or "mountain climbing" necessary.

That is not the case with many of Mount Elbert's brethren in the West. The most accessible highpoints elsewhere over 10,000 feet are in the desert southwest. Wheeler Peak (13,161 feet) in New Mexico and Boundary Peak (13,143 feet) in Arizona are both conquerable by your dog.

Moving east, the jewel for Highpointers in the Great Plains is South Dakota's Harney Peak that lords over the Black Hills. At 7,242 feet, Harney is the highest point in America east of the Rocky Mountains. The canine ascent is steady but easily manageable for your dog, with plenty of sitting room among the craggy rocks at the peak.

East of the Mississippi River there isn't a state high point your dog can't reach, save those on private or dog-restricted land. Of course, you don't need to climb at all on many - you can drive close to the top and take a short walk to the summit. Some of the famous auto mountain climbs are on Mount Washington (6,288 feet) in New Hamsphire , Mount Greylock (3,491 feet) in Massachusetts and Mount Mitchell (6,684 feet - the highest point east of the Mississippi) in North Carolina.

The smaller Eastern states also make it easier to tag several state highpoints on the same trip. In southwestern Pennsylvania your dog can make an easy one-mile hike to conquer Mount Davis (3,213 feet) then travel a few hours south to Backbone Mountain (3,360 feet) in Maryland. After you make the climb up an old fire road don't forget to sign the book with your dog's name and pick up a certificate validating his accomplishment. Next toodle over to Spruce Knob (4,863 feet) in West Virginia for a pleasant half-mile stroll from the parking lot atop the mountain to the actual summit.

So what about Florida, with the lowest "highpoint" in the nation?

The roof of Florida is at Britton Hill in Lakewood Park (off SR 285, south of Florala, Alabama). The 345-foot "summit" is scarcely twenty yards from the parking lot, marked by a granite monument. There are short paths through the nearby pine forest where your dog can walk off her excitement or just indulge in a game of fetch of instead.

Camping With Your Dog In Northwest Florida

Augie's World Campground & RV Park
Youngstown
At 2827 SR 20 W, east of intersection with Route 231.
RV/tent   **open year-round**   **(850) 674-3460**

Campers Inn
Panama City Beach
At 8800 Thomas Drive off CR 3033 from US 98.
RV/tent   **open year round**   **(850) 234-5731**

El Governor RV Park
Mexico Beach
1700 US 98 at the junction with 17th Street.
RV only   **open year-round**   **(850) 648-5432**

Emerald Coast RV Beach Resort
Panama City Beach
On US 98/98A at Allison Avenue, 1.5 miles west of Hathaway Bridge.
RV only   **open year-round**   **(850) 235-0924**

Islander RV Park
Panama City
At 2600 Highway 98.
RV only   **open year-round**   **(850) 648-4006**

Magnolia Beach RV Park
Panama City Beach - bay
At 7800 Magnolia Beach Road, east of Thomas Drive, south of US 98 .
RV only   **open year-round**   **(850) 235-1581**

Navarre Beach Campground

Panama City Beach
At 9201 Navarre Parkway, US 98, 1.5 miles east of SR 87.
RV/tent   open year-round   (850) 939-2188

Panama City Beach RV Resort

Panama City Beach
At 4702 Thomas Drive off CR 3033 from US 98.
RV only   open year-round   (850) 249-7352

Park Place

Panama City Beach
At 9322 Front Beach Road, US 98a, 2 miles west of hathaway Bridge.
RV/tent   open year-round   (850) 234-2278

Pine Lake RV Park

Fountain
North of town at 21036 US Highway 231.
RV only   open year-round   (850) 722-1401

Pineglen Motorcoach and RV Park

Panama City Beach
At 11930 Panama City Beach Parkway.
RV only   open year-round   (850) 230-8535

Raccoon River Campground

Panama City Beach
South from US 98 on Clara Road and east on Middle Beach Road to 12209.
RV/tent   open year-round   (850) 234-0181

St. Andrews State Park

Panama City
3 miles east of town off Thomas Drive, SR 392.
RV/tent   open year-round   (850) 233-5140

All-Star RV Park

Perdido Key
At 13621 Perdido Key Drive (Route 292) from I-110.
RV only   **open year-round**   **(850) 492-0041**

Big Lagoon State Park

Pensacola
From US 98 take Route 293 (Bauer Road) south to 12301 Gulf Beach Highway.
RV/tent   **open year-round**   **(850) 492-1595**

Heritage Oaks RV Park

Pensacola
At 1523 Gulf Beach Highway, SR 292, west of I-110.
RV only   **open year-round**   **(850) 455-8737**

Lake Stone Campground

Century
East of town at 801 Highway 4.
RV/tent   **open year-round**   **(850) 256-5555**

Lakeside at Barth

Molino
North of town at 855 Barth Road, east of SR 29.
RV/tent   **open year-round**   **(850) 587-2322**

Lakeside Ponds

Pensacola
At 5565 W Nine Mile Road, US 90, just east of SR 99.
RV only   **open year-round**   **(850) 944-1097**

Playa Del Rio RV Park

Perdido Key
At 16990 Perdido Key Drive, about 6 miles from Perdido Key Bridge.
RV only   **open year-round**   **(850) 492-0904**

Tall Oaks Campground RV Park

Pensacola

At 9301 Pine Forest Road, SR 297, just north of I-10, Exit 7.

RV only   **open year-round**   **(850) 479-3212**

Franklin County

Carrabelle Palms RV Park

Carrabelle

At 1843 Highway 98 West, three miles west of junction with CR 67.

RV/tent   **open year-round**   **(850) 697-2638**

Ho–Hum RV Park

Carrabelle

At 2132 Highway 98 East.

RV only   **open year-round**   **(850) 697-3926**

Gadsden County

Beaver Lake Campground

Quincy

From I-10 take Exit 174-Hwy. 12 to 133 Kneeology Way.

RV only   **open year-round**   **(850) 856-9095**

Ho–Hum RV Park

Carrabelle

At 2132 Highway 98 East.

RV only   **open year-round**   **(850) 697-3926**

Whippoorwill Sportsman Lodge

Quincy

At 3129 Cooks Landing Road, east of SR 267.

RV/tent   **open year-round**   **(850) 875-2605**

Dead Lakes State Recreation Area
Wewahitchka
North of town at 510 Gary Rowell Road, east of SR 71.
RV/tent   open year-round   (850) 639-2702

Indian Swamp Campground RV Park
Howard Creek
Off SR 71, north of US 98; east on Doc Whitefield Road to Howard Creek Road.
RV only   open year-round   (850) 827-7261

Parker Farm Campground
Wewahitchka
West on SR 22 from SR 71, south of SR 20.
RV only   open year-round   (850) 639-520

RV Camper Hideaway at Stirling Square
Ponce DeLeon
I-10. Exit 331 to US 90, and left on 83 for 9 miles to blinking light and right on CR 185; on the right after 10 miles.
RV/tent   open year-round   (850) 956-2224

Arrowhead Campsites
Marianna
At 4820 on Highway 90 east of town.
RV only   open year-round   (850) 482-558

Dove Rest RV Park & Campground
Marianna
At 1973 Dove Rest Drive, 1 mile south of I-10, Exit 142
RV/tent   open year-round   (850) 482-5313

Florida Caverns State Park

Marianna

At 3345 Caverns Road, 3 miles north of I-10, Exit US 90 on CR 166.

RV/tent   **open year-round**   **(850) 482-1228**

Three Rivers State Park

Sneads

2 miles north of town on SR 271 at 7908 Three Rivers Park Road.

RV/tent   **open year-round**   **(850) 482-9006**

Jefferson County

A Campers World RV Park

Lamont

At 397 Campground Road on US 19, just north of I-10, Exit 225.

RV only   **open year-round**   **(850) 997-3300**

Tallahassee East KOA

Monticello

On SR 259, off CR 158B, 2 miles west of US 19; south of I-10 at Exit 225.

RV/tent   **open year-round**   **(850) 997-3890**

Leon County

Bennetts Overnight Park

Tallahassee

South of I-10 on Mission Road off Route 90, West Tennessee Street, west of FSU

RV only   **open year-round**   **(904) 576-2306**

Big Oak RV Park

Tallahassee

At 4024 N. Monroe Street, Exit 199 off I-10 and go north.

RV only   **open year round**   **(850) 562-4660**

Lakeside Travel Park

Tallahassee

At 6401 W Tennessee Street, US 90, south from I-10, Exit 192.

RV only   **open year-round**   **(850) 574-5998**

Tallahassee RV Park
Tallahassee
At 6504 Mahan Drive, west of I-10 at Exit 209A.
RV only   open year-round   (850) 878-7641

Camel Lake Campground/Apalachicola National Forest
Bristol
South of town on SR 105 off Route 12.
Tent only   open year round   (850) 523-8500

Cotton Landing Campground/ Apalachicola National Forest
Sumatra
Forest Route 123B off FR123, 1 mile west of CR 379 north of town.
Tent   open year-round   (850) 523-8500

Hickory Landing/ Apalachicola National Forest
Sumatra
South of town on SR 65 and west on Forest Route 101.
RV/tent   open year-round   (850) 523-8500

Hitchcock Lake/ Apalachicola National Forest
Telogia
South of Polar Camp on CR 67 and east on Forest Route 184.
RV/tent   open year-round   (850) 523-850

Torreya State Park
Bristol
On CR 1641 off SR 12, 13 miles north of town.
RV/tent   open year-round   (850) 643-2674

Whitehead Lake/ Apalachicola National Forest
Telogia
8 miles south of town on SR 67.
RV/tent   open year-round   (850) 523-8500

Wright Lake/ Apalachicola National Forest

Sumatra

On Forest Road 101/101B, 2 miles wes tof SR 65.

RV/tent   **open year-round**   **(850) 523-8500**

Okaloosa County

Action on Blackwater Canoe Rental and Campground

Baker

On State Road at river, 4 miles west of town.

RV only - no outside pets   open year-round   (850) 537-2997

Bayview Campground

Destin

On Joes Bayou at 749 Beach Drive off Route 98 (Harbor Boulevard)

RV and tent   open year-round   (850) 837-5085

Camping On The Gulf Holiday Travel Park

Destin

At 10005 Emerald Coast Parkway (US 98), 4.6 miles east of SR 293

RV/tent   open year round   (850) 837-6334

Crystal Beach Campground

Destin

At 2825 Highway 98.

RV/tent   open year-round   (850) 837-6447

Destin RV Beach Resort

Destin

362 Miramar Beach Drive, four miels east of Mid-Bay Bridge.

RV only   open year-round   (850) 837-3529

Destin RV Resort

Destin

150 Regions Way, south of US 98, just east of SR 293.

Rv/tent   open year-round   (850) 837-6215

Eagle's Landing RV Park
Holt
At 4504 Log Lake Road, just north of I-10, Exit 45.
RV only   open year-round   (850) 537-9657

Fred Gannon Rocky Bayou State Park
Niceville
On Highway 20, 5 miles east of Highway 85.
RV/tent   open year-round   (850) 833-9144

Geronimo RV Resort
Destin
At 75 Arnett Lane, 3 miles east of town between US 98 and Scenic Hwy 98.
RV only   open year-round   (850) 424-6801

Holiday Lakes Travel Park
Crestview
4050 S Ferdon Boulevard, SR 85, just south of I-10, Exit 56.
RV only   open year-round   (850) 682-6377

Playground RV Park
Fort Walton Beach
At 777 Beal Parkway, SR 189, from SR 393, north of US 98.
RV only   open year-round   (850) 862-3513

River's Edge RV Campground
Holt
At 4001 Log Lake Road, just north of I-10, Exit 45.
RV only   open year-round   (850) 537-4544

Santa Rosa County

Adventures Unlimited Outdoor Center – NO DOGS!

Blackwater River State Park
Holt
From Exit 31 of I-10 go north to US 90 and head east to Deaton Bridge Road on th eleft and continue to park at 7720.
RV/tent   open year-round   (850) 983-5363

By the Bay RV Park
Milton
From I-10, Exit 22, go south on Avalon boulevard (Route 281) and turn right on Pearson road and right on Michael Drive to 5550.
RV/tent   **open year-round**   (850) 623-0262

Cedar Pines RV Campground
Milton
Four miles north of SR 90 on SR 87 at 6436 Roble Road.
RV/tent   **open year-round**   (850) 623-8869

Emerald Beach RV Park
Navarre
At 8885 Navarre Parkway, US 98, just east of junction with SR 87 .
RV only   **open year-round**   (850) 939-3431

Grayton Beach State Park
Santa Rosa Beach
On CR 30A, just south of US 98.
RV/tent   **open year-round**   (850) 231-4210

Gulf Pines KOA
Milton
At 8700 Gulf Pines Drive just north of I-10, Exit 31.
RV/tent   **open year-round**   (850) 623-0808

Peach Creek RV Park
Santa Rosa Beach
At 4401 East Highway 98.
RV only   **open year-round**   (850) 231-1948

Pelican Palms RV Park
Milton
At 3700 Garcon Point Road, just north of I-10, Exit 26.
RV/tent   **open year-round**   (850) 623-0576

Topsail Hill Preserve State Park
Santa Rosa Beach
On Route 30A, 1 mile off US 98.
RV only   **open year-round**   (850) 267-0299

Holiday Campground
Panacea
On US 98 at northeast end of Panacea Bridge.
RV/tent   **open year-round**   **(850) 984-5757**

Ochlockonee River State Park
Sopchoppy
On US 319, 4 miles south of town.
RV/tent   **open year-round**   **(850) 962-2771**

Lazy Days RV Park
Freeport
At 18655 on US 331, 2.5 miles south of the junction with SR 20.
RV only   **open year-round**   **(850) 835-4606**

Longleaf RV Park
De Funiak Springs
At 5635 on Highway 331, 3.5 miles south of I-10, Exit 85.
RV only   **open year-round**   **(850) 892-7261**

Sunset King Lake Resort
De Funiak Springs
At 366 Paradise Island Drive off Kings Lake Road off SR 331.
RV only   **open year-round**   **(850) 892-7229**

Falling Waters State Park
Chipley
1130 State Park Road off SR 77, 3 miles south of town.
RV/tent   **open year-round**   **(850) 638-6130**

Your Dog At The Beach

It is hard to imagine many places a dog is happier than at a beach. Whether romping on the sand, digging a hole, jumping in the water or just lying in the sun, every dog deserves a day at the beach. Except in Florida.

But slowly the "NO DOGS ON BEACH" signs are starting to come down in some spots around the state. On the Gulf Coast in Northwest Florida a dog beach opened in 2007 on city property in Panama City Beach. You can find this sliver of tail-friendly sand, open to residents and visitors alike, to the west of the Dan Russell Pier (on Front Beach Road, just east of the junction with SR 79). For canine hikers this is a fortuitous location as it welds a link between the waves of the Gulf of Mexico across to Frank Brown Park, where dog lovers will find more than a mile of pathways and a fenced dog park. Frank Brown Park is also a launching spot for *Gayle's Trails*, a network of paved paths that span the entire island east from St. Andrews Beach to the new Pines and Ponds being developed across SR 79. When completed in 2008 this untouched 3,000-acre paradise once owned by the St. Joe Company will be open to canine hiking on miles of upland dirt trails.

Another place your dog can test the warm waters of the Gulf of Mexico is at a rest stop west of Carrabelle Beach in Franklin County. Although the waves are tamed in St. Geoge Sound by barrier islands your dog isn't likely to complain.

Index To Parks, Trails & Open Space

Bay County
	page
Camp Helen State Park	36
Econfina Creek Water Management Area	100
Pine Lake State Forest	34
St. Andrews State Park	70

Escambia County
	page
Big Lagoon State Park	76
Tarkiln Bayou State Park	62
University of West Florida	96

Franklin County
	page
Bald Point State Park	64
Box-R Wildlife Management Area	100
St. George Island State Park	60
Tate's Hell State Forest	26

Gadsden County
	page
Bear Creek Educational Forest	26
Joe Budd Wildlife Management Area	99

Gulf County
	page
Dead Lakes State Recreation Area	101
St. Joseph Bay State Buffer Preserve	92
St. Joseph Peninsula State Park	78

Holmes County
	page
Henderson Beach State Park	90
Ponce de Leon Springs State Park	68

Jackson County
	page
Florida Caverns State Park	32
Three Rivers State Park	68

Jefferson County
	page
Aucilla Wildlife Management Area	97
St. Marks National Wildlife Refuge	22

Leon County
	page
Alfred B. Maclay Gardens State Park	58
Apalachicola National Forest	30
Elinor Klapp-Phipps Park	38
Fort Braden Trails	48
J.R. Alford Greenway	44
Lake Jackson Mounds State Park	82
Leon Sinks Geological Area	20
Miccosukee Canopy Road Greenway	50
Tallahassee-St. Marks Trail	94
Tom Brown Park	98

Liberty County
	page
Apalachicola National Forest	30
Torreya State Park	16

Okaloosa County
	page
Blackwater River State Forest	28
Fred Gannon Rocy Bayou State Park	86

Santa Rosa County
	page
Blackwater Heritage State Trail	84
Blackwater River State Forest	28
Blackwater River State Park	74
Deer Lake State Park	99
Fort Pickens	80
Garcon Point Trails	70
Naval Live Oaks	24

Taylor County

	page
Aucilla Wildlife Management Area	97
Econfina River State Park	66

Wakulla County

	page
Apalachicola National Forest	30
Ochlockonee River State Park	56
St. Marks National Wildlife Refuge	22
Tallahassee-St. Marks Trail	94
Wakulla Springs State Park	54

Walton County

	page
Eden Gardens State Park	72
Grayton Beach State Park	40
Lakewood Park	103
Point Washington State Forest	52
Topsail Hill Preserve State Park	18

Washington County

	page
Econfina Creek Water Management Area	100
Falling Waters State Park	46
Pine Log State Forest	34

How To Pet A Dog
Tickling tummies slowly and gently works wonders.
Never use a rubbing motion; this makes dogs bad-tempered.
A gentle tickle with the tips of the fingers is all that is necessary
to induce calm in a dog. I hate strangers who go up to dogs with their
hands held to the dog's nose, usually palm towards themselves.
How does the dog know that the hand doesn't hold something horrid?
The palm should always be shown to the dog and go straight
down to between the dog's front legs and tickle gently with
a soothing voice to accompany the action.
Very often the dog raises its back leg in a scratching movement,
it gets so much pleasure from this.
-Barbara Woodhouse

Other Books On Hiking With Your Dog from Cruden Bay Books
www.hikewithyourdog.com

DOGGIN' THE MID-ATLANTIC: *400 Tail-Friendly Parks To Hike With Your Dog In New Jersey, Pennsylvania, Delaware, Maryland and Northern Virginia - $18.95*
DOGGIN' THE POCONOS: *The 33 Best Places To Hike With Your Dog In Pennsylvania's Northeast Mountains - $9.95*
DOGGIN' THE BERKSHIRES: *The 33 Best Places To Hike With Your Dog In Western Massachusetts - $9.95*
DOGGIN' NORTHERN VIRGINIA: *The 50 Best Places To Hike With Your Dog In NOVA - $9.95*
DOGGIN' DELAWARE: *The 40 Best Places To Hike With Your Dog In The First State - $9.95*
DOGGIN' MARYLAND: *The 100 Best Places To Hike With Your Dog In The Free State - $12.95*
DOGGIN' JERSEY: *The 100 Best Places To Hike With Your Dog In The Garden State - $12.95*
DOGGIN' RHODE ISLAND: *The 25 Best Places To Hike With Your Dog In The Ocean State - $7.95*
DOGGIN' THE FINGER LAKES: *The 50 Best Places To Hike With Your Dog - $12.95*
DOGGIN' CONNECTICUT: *The 57 Best Places To Hike With Your Dog In The Nutmeg State - $12.95*
DOGGIN' LONG ISLAND: *The 30 Best Places To Hike With Your Dog In New York's Playground - $9.95*
DOGGIN' THE TIDEWATER: *The 33 Best Places To Hike With Your Dog from the Northern Neck to Virginia Beach - $9.95*
DOGGIN' THE CAROLINA COASTS: *The 50 Best Places To Hike With Your Dog Along The North Carolina And South Carolina Shores - $11.95*
DOGGIN' AMERICA'S BEACHES: *A Traveler's Guide To Dog-Friendly Beaches - (and those that aren't) - $12.95*
THE CANINE HIKER'S BIBLE - $19.95
A Bark In The Park: The 55 Best Places To Hike With Your Dog In The Philadelphia Region - $12.95
A Bark In The Park: The 50 Best Places To Hike With Your Dog In The Baltimore Region - $12.95
A Bark In The Park: The 37 Best Places To Hike With Your Dog In Pennsylvania Dutch Country - $9.95

CPSIA information can be obtained at www.ICGtesting.com
Printed in the USA
LVOW01s1818200315

431395LV00016B/697/P